Praise for *I'll Meet You at the Base of the Mountain*

"In this powerful and riveting book, Donna generously shares her heroic journey through one of the most searingly painful lessons about life, loss, and heartbreak a person, and mother can ever face. This book will touch your soul to the core, walking you through some of our deepest fears and into the brightest healing light of love and understanding that the spirit never dies. You must read it!"

- **Sonia Choquette**, NY Times Best Selling Author of *The Answer is Simple...Love Yourself Live Your Spirit*

"A beautifully written, refreshingly real account from a woman who turned tragedy into lessons all of us can never hear too often. Perfect for any parent who has lost a child or anyone whose soul needs a heavenly lift."

- **Suzanne Giesemann**, author of *Messages of Hope*

"In this bittersweet tribute, Donna Visocky generously shares her heart-breaking story with the world, yet tells it with such tenderness and finesse. This book is a treasure trove for those of us trying to survive and make sense of grief. Read it and celebrate this tale of courage. Let Donna be your guide as we all learn to navigate the bittersweet mysteries of life, death, and how life endures even after death—both for us and for the ones we love. Donna's first book is a triumph and Donna Visocky is an inspiration!"

- **Amelia Kinkade**, Author of *Straight From the Horse's Mouth: How to Talk to Animals and Get Answers, Soulmates with Paws, Hooves, and Wings, Aurora's Secret,* and *The Winged One*

"Donna has written a powerful and poignant transcript of personal transformation. Her personal journey beautifully shows us how tragedy can lead to living an extraordinary and fulfilling life. This is inspired writing."

- **Cynthia James**, Author, speaker, teacher

"I began working with Donna Visocky and BellaSpark Productions in 2010. Donna had shared with me her story and what an amazing story it was! To now read the words and realize how far Donna and her family have come, is so heartwarming and demonstrates to us the power of the human spirit and the power of love. It reminds us that we are never alone and that there is always a way out of the depths of grief & sorrow when we lose a loved one. It's truly been a pleasure to work with Donna and witness first-hand her strength and determination to make this work available to empower others."

- **Dr Joe Dispenza**

"I'll Meet You at the Base of the Mountain *is an inspirational story that will bring comfort to many people!"*

\- **John Holland**, Author of *The Spirit Whisper: Chronicles of a Medium*

"I'll Meet You at the Base of the Mountain *describes the personal journey of a mother after the death of her daughter. It beautifully weaves the transformation of her life with the journey of discovering how the love of her daughter, Kristi, lives on and continues to touch many lives. She traveled every road, tirelessly searching every avenue — spiritual and scientific — to learn that death is not the end, only the beginning . . . a new way to connect with her daughter. Kristi's essence and memory continue to live on and touch thousands of lives. This book is a must-read for anyone grappling with birth and death and wondering if love does indeed go on."*

\- **Suzane Northrop**, Internationally-Acclaimed Medium, Grief & Bereavement Expert, TV and Radio host and author of *Second Chance: Healing Messages from the Afterlife, Everything Happens for a Reason: Love, Free Will & Lessons of the Soul* and *A Medium's Cookbook: Recipes for the Soul*

"During my career, I have read hundreds of books based on life after death, and people's memoirs of those they have loved and who have passed into spirit. I have also had the pleasure to know Donna personally. Her book is an incredible memoir of her daughter, but also shows her struggle with the "woo woo," the same struggle I went through in my early years. What a book! I could not stop reading it — a simply wonderful, amazing book. Donna, thank you for finally writing the book, I know it will be an inspiration to many souls, who like you, have been looking for answers about life after death."

\- **Margaret McElroy**, channel, author, and teacher

"I'll Meet You at the Base of the Mountain *offers spiritual life lessons that can be shared with people of all ages and faiths. A journey of courage and sharing from the other side."*

\- **Gary Quinn**, bestselling author of *TheYes Frequency* and *May The Angels Be With You*

"Donna Visocky shares her journey in a way that brings you to an understanding that both life and death have a destination and when you allow yourself to take the journey of understanding its purpose, you awaken the part of you that you closed."

\- **Kimmie Rose Zapf**, internationally renowned intuitive, medium, hypnotherapist, author, speaker and radio host

I'll Meet You at the Base of the Mountain

One woman's journey from grief to life.

Donna Visocky

Some names and identifying details have been changed to protect the
confidentiality of the individuals involved.
When actual names have been used,
permission has been granted.

Published by BellaSpark Press: BellaSpark Productions
www.BellaSpark.com

ISBN: 978-0-9899335-0-6

Library of Congress Control # 2013917041

Cover and interior design by ADS, Inc.

Dedication

To my husband Bob and my children Jason, Adam, and Jenny — you gave me a foundation on which to stand allowing me to spread my wings.

To my three beautiful grandchildren Nicholas, Drew, and Hampton — you are my greatest teachers.

To the many beautiful souls who have shared this journey with me, supporting me, encouraging me, inspiring me — I am blessed to have you in my life.

Most of all to Kristi — through your death, I have been born again.

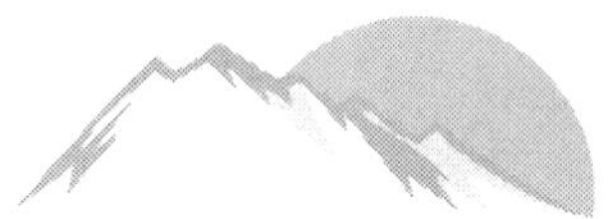

Contents

Foreword

By Alan Cohen

All great spiritual masters have told us that it is not the events that occur in life that determine our success and happiness, but what we make of them. That's an easy platitude to agree with, but when hardships come our way, we discover where we believe our well-being lives.

When Donna Visocky's daughter Kristi was killed in a car crash, Donna had no idea how her life would change as a result of that experience. *No idea.* Of course she had to face and work through the deep grief that any human being in that situation must contend with. Her process was not easy and she had to peel away the pain and sorrow layer by layer.

Yet on the other side of that dark tunnel was a light. Donna began to ask questions deeper and more profound than she had previously considered. *Is there life after death? Is Kristi still alive somewhere? Can I communicate with her?* And the more pervasive inquiries: *Why am I here? What am I supposed to be doing with my life? Is there a Higher Power that I can communicate with and receive guidance from? How is my path connected to the paths that others walk?*

The powerful effect of asking big questions like these is that they lead to big answers. They lead to profound life changes. They lead to healing. They lead to peace.

In *I'll Meet You at the Base of the Mountain*, Donna Visocky nakedly shares her journey from grief to healing; from fear to love; from the dark night of the soul to the vision from the mountaintop. Her odyssey is important not simply for the fascinating and uncanny experiences she has had, including signs and messages from Kristi, but for her adventure's relevance to *all of us*. Though we may not have lost a child, we have all experienced the pain of loss and wondered why we are here and what it will take for us to find peace. Donna maps a journey we all walk: from the pain of loss and separation to the clarity of our spiritual wholeness.

But the story doesn't end there. The healing and expansion that Donna found has ultimately affected many thousands, perhaps millions, of people beyond herself. Through establishing Bella Spark Productions and offering the many lectures, seminars, and magazine issues the company has produced, the lessons of life beyond death have come to uplift the world. *A Course in Miracles* tells us, "When I am healed I am not healed alone." Now, through *I'll Meet You at the Base of the Mountain* Donna Visocky's healing becomes yours, and mine, and all who are open to receive it.

This is not a book about psychic phenomena. This is a guide to spiritual awakening. I am so pleased that Donna has taken pen to paper and recorded her experiences and the important lessons she has gleaned. I know that Kristi is proud, smiling down upon Donna from where she now sits, as your loved ones smile upon you and seek to help you find the peace you so richly deserve, and shall surely have.

Alan Cohen

Preface

"Kristi came to me this morning. She has a message for you."

The email came from a woman I had just met a week before. Kimmie Rose Zapf is a psychic medium from Michigan. We met at a book event in Denver and immediately hit it off. I was surprised to hear from her and especially to hear that Kristi had visited her.

"She said she will meet you at the base of the mountain."

Kimmie went on to describe the mountain: tall and lush and green with huge boulder outcrops. At the base was a river. That was it.

Where is this mountain Kristi? What do you want me to do? I can't imagine where this mountain might be, but I would do anything to find it. I want to meet you there. My heart is breaking, I so long to connect with you. Please show me where it is, Kristi.

I am getting ahead of myself.

In 2003 my daughter Kristi was killed in a car accident. She was 21 years old. Her death sent me on a search for answers. *Why did this happen to us? Is she ok? Where does one go when they die? Can I communicate with her?* Kristi's death led me on an amazing journey, one I could never have imagined, to places beyond my comprehension and experiences that are out of this world.

There is life after death.

How do I know? Do I have proof? Maybe not the tangible kind those with an analytical mind might require. But all that I have experienced over the past ten years leaves no doubt in my mind that life does go on, that we are always connected to not only our loved ones but the divine energy of God and can tap into it ourselves whenever we are ready. I know that death is not the end, merely the conclusion of one tiny scene in a never-ending performance called life.

When someone you love dies, it is as if you have been thrown into an abyss so deep and dark the sun cannot reach you. How does one even begin to pull oneself out of such deep despair? No footholds, nothing to grab onto. You are lost. You ask yourself, *do I even want to?* Perhaps I will stay in this place of darkness forever.

The interesting thing is life won't let you stay there. You do not belong in the darkness, and so day by day, week by week, months and then years later, you find your way back. Only the world looks different now, because you are different, better maybe. The fabric of your life is richer, fuller, and more vibrant. You begin to learn who you are and find a new purpose, one that never would have shown itself if you had not experienced what you had. It is a purpose that is so much larger and grander than anything you could have imagined.

Yes, there is a life after death.

This is my story . . .

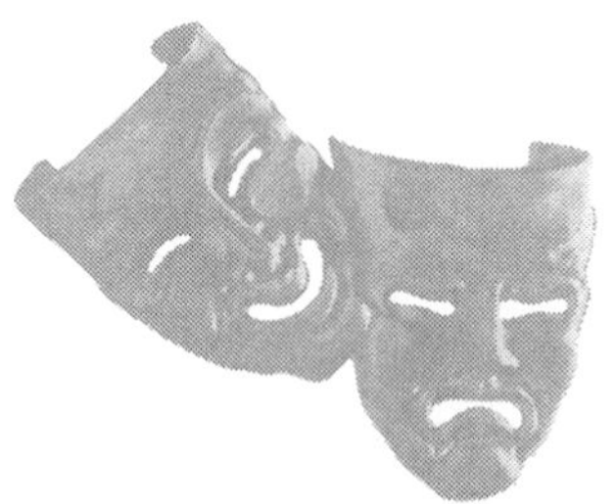

- The Mask -

When you lose someone you love, it's like a light goes out in your heart. When my daughter, Kristi, died, I felt that the light in my soul would never shine again. But life goes on, they say, and you have things to do. So you put on your mask and face the world everyday. The mask hides the pain and the grief on your face, in your heart; and you get through the day. The mask becomes a new part of you and you are prepared to wear it forever.

And then little things happen.

- You see a sign—a butterfly or a penny, and you know that she is with you and always will be a part of you

. . . and the mask begins to crack.

- My grandson Nicholas tells me he sees Aunt Kristi. "She is the brightest star in the sky," he says. And you know that she gently guides him

. . . and the mask cracks a little more until a faint light, your light, shines weakly through.

- My friend Rayno says Kristi's smiling face pops into his mind and brightens his day. And you know that she made an impact on people

. . . and the cracks in the mask grow wider; and the light peeks through, like rays of sun partially hidden behind a cloud.

- My beautiful daughter Jenny gives birth to my new granddaughter, and you know that she is sent to you as a gift from God and Kristi to ease your pain

... and the cracks grow even wider as you dare to allow your love and light to shine on this new child.

And so it goes . . .

Slowly, little by little, the mask breaks apart and you begin to feel the sun on your face again; the light in your heart shine again. It may take years, but you know that someday, some how, the mask will disintegrate and you will show your face to the world again. It is a different face than before, because you are different, but it will be your face, none-the-less, and not the mask.

– Donna Visocky

CHAPTER 1

The Doorbell

"Sorrow you can hold, however desolating,
if nobody speaks to you.
If they speak, you break down."
~Bede Jarrett

The doorbell rings at 5:30 a.m., jarring me out of a sound sleep. Jumping up, still in my pajamas, I glance out the kitchen window. Seeing two squad cars, my heart stops.

They stand tentatively on my front step, two police officers and a third man wearing a chaplain badge on his shirt pocket. That badge. It is seared into my memory like a hot branding iron, imprinted forever onto my brain.

"Bob, get up. And put some pants on!" I yell to my husband before any of them can speak. It's funny where your mind goes, even as your world is falling apart around you. I know this is going to be one of those life-defining moments; I don't want my husband to remember it as him standing there in his boxers.

I let them stand there on the front stoop, none of us saying a word. Though I am quiet, my mind is screaming, *"Don't let them in. Don't let them in! They can't say what they came to say if we don't let them in."*

"This can't be good," my husband says, the blood draining from his face as he takes a look at the threesome at our door. Then he lets them in.

"Do you have a daughter named Kristi?" asks the tall one.

Suddenly I know my life will never be the same. My daughter died in an auto accident that night, on her way home from an evening with friends, just a mile from her apartment. They say most accidents happen within a three-mile radius of home; Kristi is one of those statistics. She was 21 years old.

We learn that Kristi died in a single car accident in south Denver, in a construction zone, part of the huge T-Rex project to redo the freeway. It was late, around 2:00 a.m., the area a confusing maze of lane closures, detours, and equipment. She drove straight into the back of a blockade truck, they tell us. She died instantly, blunt force trauma to the head.

"Do you want someone to stay with you for a while until your family arrives?" the chaplain asks.

"Please leave. We will be okay."

We do not want to spend any more time in their presence. Bob calls our other children, our sons, Jason and Adam, and our daughter Jenny. I call my sister Mary. They show up, one by one, with a look of disbelief on their faces.

I hand my sister my address book and leave her the difficult job of contacting the rest of the family. I am reminded of when my father died. I was fifteen. With no other family close, it fell to my mother to call the relatives and give them the news. One call after another, it was painful to watch her recount the same story over and over. Mary steps into that role for us, making the necessary calls to family and friends.

We ask each other who else needs to know. We settle on a few close friends, and again my sister tracks them down and makes the calls. Pretty soon the house is full of people as the word quickly spreads. I finally get in the shower, knowing that soon we will be inundated with people; time to clean up and put on my face. It's a mask I will be wearing for a long time.

Somewhere in the back of my mind it dawns on me that I am supposed to meet a friend for coffee this morning. I am sure she is already sitting at the coffee shop, wondering where I am. I don't know how to reach her. *I hope she understands.*

That evening, while silently watching the news on television, we see the report of the accident: her car, twisted and mangled, the coroner rolling a body bag into the back of a van. It is like watching a bad movie, surreal. *This can't be our daughter.*

There are so many questions, so many details to take care of. I think of the funeral parlor I drive by every day on the way to work and there is another just a couple blocks from my office. *We can't go there; I do not want to be reminded every day.* We settle on a small place tucked back in an industrial park. *I will never have to see these people again.*

We have not been active in our church but my friend Mary Jo offers to help coordinate the funeral. She asks her sons, four gifted musicians, to do the music.

My friend Karen works for a photographer; she asks me for my favorite photo of Kristi and takes it to him so it can be blown up for the funeral. She brings it back in a nice black frame.

We call our insurance agent. He says not to worry about a thing. He will take care of everything. And he does. What a blessing.

I am grateful for the support and kindness, but mostly I just want to be left alone.

At the funeral Jason, my oldest child, is the stoic one, keeping his emotions in check, in a state of readiness in case I do something foolish like lose control and throw myself on the coffin. Adam, always the hugger in the family, stays close, available to wrap his arms around me when needed. Jenny is the only one who has the courage to speak, calmly sharing stories, insights, and escapades about her little sister who was often a thorn in her side growing up. I am amazed at how strong she is; I can feel her grief and disbelief. None of them expected to be in this place of losing a sister. Something like this is not supposed to happen to us.

The chaplain is there. He no longer wears the badge, but I recognize that face. How dare he show up at this sacred time. He keeps trying to talk to me, to offer his condolences or something. I turn away, refusing to look at him. I will not allow this bringer of bad news to enter my world a second time.

CHAPTER 2
Kristi

"Angels come to visit us,
and we only know them when they are gone."
-Author Unknown

The youngest of my four children, Kristi was my baby. With two brothers, Jason and Adam, nine and seven years older, and a sister, Jenny, four years older, Kristi instinctively knew she had to be loud and demanding to establish her place in our busy family. And demanding she was. I felt like she was attached to my hip at times. She loved to sleep in my bed with me when her dad was out of town.

As I look back now with new eyes after all I have learned these past few years, I realize Kristi was very intuitive. At two she would declare, "Answer the door. Isn't anyone going to answer the door?" A minute or two later the doorbell would chime. Same with the phone—we always knew when a call was coming in; Kristi would announce it before the phone even started its ringing. I suspect she saw things at night alone in her bed—spirits, ghosts, others—things that frightened her. She would come to me in the middle of the night to ask if I would sleep with her. I would curl up next to her, wrapping my arms around her, gently stroking her blond hair, caressing her face. It was a ritual we repeated often, even as she grew to be a teenager when the burdens of her life were too heavy to carry alone. It was a rite I did before her funeral, before they took her away from me for good, as I sat next to her silent casket.

"It's okay, baby. I'm here. I love you," I whispered —the same words I said to her over the years, my one final act of love.

She was a lonely child, not really connecting with kids her own age. As if she didn't quite belong in this often harsh world that didn't live up to her expectations. More comfortable with adults, Kristi would often head to the neighbor kids' house to play only to end up sitting at the kitchen table talking with their parents.

When Kristi was in kindergarten we were called to a meeting with the principal. Kristi had pushed and punched a boy on the playground.

"But he was picking on Tommy," Kristi declared. Tommy was a handicapped child, the one no one would play with. Kristi became his protector and playmate. Her first grade teacher once told us, "If this was the '60s, Kristi would be leading the protest."

In junior high, an age when raging hormones and teenage insecurities turn children into unrecognizable creatures, Kristi struggled to fit in. It broke my heart when she came home from school in tears because no one would sit with her at lunch. One teacher took Kristi under her wing and invited her to eat lunch with her in the music room. Thank you, Miss Shelly. Later I would learn about Indigo Children—Kristi was a classic early Indigo. Strong, outspoken, sensitive to the feelings of others, angry about the injustices in the world, she didn't put up with the not-so-nice games the kids played, and thus they didn't like her. Life can be cruel to a sensitive soul.

As she grew older, she tended to collect lost kids, those with overwhelming issues of their own. The young girl whose mother died, the boy who eventually committed suicide, and others—they gravitated to her, perhaps because they knew she could see the pain they held hidden deep inside and felt her willingness to ease their struggle just by being there for them, by accepting them. But the role of confidant, guide, and mentor can be difficult when you are still a child yourself.

Out of four children Kristi was the most talkative, recapping her day, espousing her opinions, arguing, and sometimes sharing too much information. She demanded a lot of my attention—more than I wanted to give at times. While her sister, Jenny, always wanted to be an only child, Kristi thrived on family interactions. When first her brothers and then her sister left home to embark on their new lives, Kristi missed the camaraderie, the pillow fights on my bed when they were home alone, the family tiffs, and just having someone else around; alone is not something she wanted to be.

Was she perfect? Hell no! Of all my children, I think Kristi gave me the most trouble. Outspoken and strong-willed, everything was intense with her. She surely was responsible for a large portion of the gray hair on my head. She did her share of partying and at the age of sixteen ran away from home. I had taken Jenny and Kristi to Puerto Vallarta, Mexico for spring break. It was a beautiful time and Kristi especially liked it, so much so that she decided life was better there than at home. It didn't take her long after our return to figure out a way to revisit—she definitely was a resourceful child. We found her two weeks later, back in Puerto Vallarta with not only a place to stay, but a job. And a couple of tattoos. Furious as I was, I began to realize how alone she must have felt. The entire time she was gone, not one person called asking for her. I'm sorry, Kristi, I didn't understand. She lay next to me again, when she was safely home, the lost child that she was. I stroked her hair and caressed her cheek, trying to convince her things would be all right—or maybe I was trying to convince myself.

Kristi was a beautiful soul shining its light in a sometimes dark, dense world. Outspoken, passionate, and spirited with a strong sense of right and wrong—how that girl loved to argue! She struggled to fit in, trying to find her place in a world that didn't match up to her values. Watching her grow up, I knew she would be an amazing woman and I wanted to be more like her. She always spoke her truth even when it got her into trouble. After her death, we heard from numerous classmates who shared how Kristi inspired them by standing up to the school bullies, those who dictated the arbitrary rules of who was cool and who wasn't. She touched many lives, most of all my own.

I found this poem Kristi had written in her things:

KRISTI
BITCHY, FLIRTATIOUS, FUN, OUTSPOKEN
SISTER OF JASON, ADAM, AND JENNY
LOVER OF MUSIC, DOLPHINS, AND MY FAMILY
WHO FEELS ALONE EACH NIGHT WHEN I GO TO SLEEP,
FEISTY WHEN I FIND SOMETHING ELSE TO ARGUE ABOUT,
AND OVERWHELMED WITH ALL THE CHOICES COMING UP IN MY LIFE.
WHO NEEDS LOTS OF ATTENTION, MY MOTHER, AND PLENTY OF SLEEP.
WHO OFFERS A SHOULDER TO CRY ON WHEN FRIENDS ARE IN NEED,
MY HEART TO THE ANIMALS AT THE HUMANE SOCIETY,
AND GIVES AN OPINION WHEN I FEEL SOMETHING IS WRONG.
WHO FEARS BEING ALONE WHEN I GROW OLD,
LOSING MY MOTHER, AND BEING ORDINARY.
WHO WOULD LIKE TO SEE MY GRANDCHILDREN BE BORN,
A WOMAN BECOME PRESIDENT,
AND TRAVEL AROUND THE WORLD.
RESIDENT OF FORT COLLINS: MAROON
VISOCKY

CHAPTER 3

Coping

"Where you used to be, there is a hole in the world, which I find myself constantly walking around in the daytime, and falling into at night. I miss you like hell."

-Edna St. Vincent Millay

I go back to work the very next week. I tell myself it is because I have much to do in my role as Executive Director of the Symphony, after all the show must go on. I work in a small two-person office and my new assistant is just starting; someone needs to train her. I know the real reason is because I can't stand to be home in my empty house all alone with my thoughts, but I pretend that my presence is extremely important. It is a skill I learn quickly, pretending.

The home phone rings; I nervously screen the caller ID. The

name says "Bonnie Cochran" and I vaguely remember she lost a son a few years prior. I let it go to voice mail.

"Just reaching out," she says. "Let me know if you want to talk." I press the delete button. The last thing I want to do is talk to someone, to share my pain.

I come home from work to find a package on my front porch. It is from the same Bonnie who left me the voice message a week ago. Inside is a little candle.

"Someone gave me one just like this when Billy died. I light it every day in memory of him," the enclosed note says.

I don't call her back, or even send her a thank you. She is another reminder that I am now part of her club, the Mother of Dead Kids Club. *I never signed up for this club. I didn't ask to be a part of this group. Screw this club!*

I light the candle anyway.

I pick a hair salon at random from the phone book and go in for a new hair cut. I had spent years trying to find just the right hairdresser—someone who understood my hair, what it would and wouldn't do, just the right cut for my face, and I had finally found her—but I can't go back. I don't want to spend an hour in close quarters with anyone, having to either share about Kristi or make uncomfortable small talk to avoid the subject. I realize that the real reason is I don't want to be me.

My friend Mary Jo stops by with a movie—*Shadowlands,* starring Anthony Hopkins and Debra Winger. It is a sad movie of love and loss and Mary Jo is unsure if it is the wise thing for me to watch, but actually it is perfect. We sit in silence, no need to talk. I cry freely without embarrassment. The tears I have been holding in check are finally released.

Tonight Bob and I are invited to our friends' home for dinner. They aren't the close kind of friends who are sensitive to and understand what we are going through. These people have no children of their own after all, but they are good people and we haven't gone out much so maybe it is time we started socializing again. Over dinner they talk about their cat that died recently—how she was with them for 10 years, how much they miss her, what a darling she was, how hard it's been on them.

Fuck the cat! my husband and I are both thinking. *It's just a stupid cat. Who the hell gives a shit?* We decide not to visit them again for a while.

Fuck is my favorite word lately. My mother would be appalled but it is the perfect word to express my anger, my rage. I use it sometimes when I rant at God, which I seem to do a lot. I take long walks on remote trails and carry on long diatribes with Him, questioning everything in the universe. *How can you allow people to feel so much pain and grief? Why don't you put a stop to war? Another parent should not lose a child ever again!* On and on, I don't know if my ranting helps or if God even cares what I think, but at least it releases some of my fury. Sometimes I drive in the car and scream at the top of my lungs. That helps a little too, or at least it allows me to put on my public face, my mask, for another while.

⸻

It has been a long week. Drained from trying to maintain my façade in front of the people I work with, I am anxious to get home and close the door on the world. Driving my usual route I pull up behind a small white car. The license plate reads I AM FORGIVEN. The car seems to be heading the same direction as me and I follow it for several miles. It is so obvious it is a message for me that I continue following even as I pass the turn to my neighborhood. I am tempted to drive around behind this car forever. I ponder the meaning. *Am I forgiven, or is Kristi the one? And what are we forgiven for? She for having an accident and leaving us, or me for being a less than perfect parent or for being mad at God?*

⸻

We paint the exterior of the house. My poor husband. It is my need to stay busy, not his. He covers the boards, I paint the trim—wordless—one board, one window at a time, pouring our grief into each brush stroke. We don't talk much, neither of us big on sharing our feelings. It is better to keep things inside, tightly controlled and contained, for I know that this pain and anguish, if ever released, would erupt like an angry volcano, spewing rage and guilt like fiery molten lava destroying everything in its path and I would be unable to recant it.

Stoic survival is a skill I learned from my mother, a strong, silent woman who carried on quietly, never complaining, despite the challenges life handed her. The ache in the pit of my stomach is a constant reminder of how empty I feel. Weekends I leave the house for hours unable to bear the pain in Bob's eyes, not sure how to help him, not wanting his fumbling efforts to comfort me. It is better to be alone. I wander aimlessly around our city's bustling downtown, seeking anonymity amidst the families having ice cream, visitors shopping and enjoying lunch at one of the outside patios, street musicians offering their music. I pray that I don't run into someone I know. If I do and am lucky enough to spot them before they see me, I craft elaborate maneuvers to avoid them, evading eye contact at all cost.

I am standing on a downtown corner waiting for the light to change when I first feel the urge. A large bus is heading my way. It would be so easy to just step in front of that bus. I can end the pain in my heart in one fell swoop. I consciously hold myself back, but not before taking one tentative step out into the street.

My son Jason decides, just days after the funeral, that we need to hold a memorial golf tournament in Kristi's name with proceeds going to a program for young people, those that she advocated for. He wants to hold it around her birthday, July 29th. Bob jumps on the idea of an annual golf tournament and fundraiser. He quickly creates a non-profit organization, the Kristi Visocky Memorial Foundation. It is his lifeline, a way to honor his daughter and bring some meaning back into his life. It gives him a new purpose.

"I do this for my daughter," he says. And though I appreciate the positive things they are creating with this event, it is difficult for me to participate and help coordinate. We have a big party on the Friday night before the tournament for all the golfers and folks from the community who graciously come out to support our cause. Bob loves it. I hate every minute of it. The idea of holding a party in honor of my dead daughter makes me sick to my stomach. It is all I can do to show up.

The tournament, just ten weeks after Kristi's death, includes 234 golfers and raises over $5000 which is donated to a program that works with at-risk youth. I am there to help with check in and details but I refuse to golf.

I join a business leadership class. I tell myself I need to keep active and stay involved in something. I sit next to a gentleman I have never met before. We do the usual small talk: Who are you? What do you do? Then he asks me if I have any children. It is the first time I am asked this question since Kristi's death. It takes me a long time to respond, so long that I am sure he wonders what is going on with this woman. *Do I say, "Yes, I have four children, two sons and two daughters?" Do I address the fact that one is dead and open that painful conversation with a total stranger? Do I only talk about the three living and ignore the beautiful part of my life that is no longer with me?* I tell him I have four children, two sons and two daughters and that my youngest daughter died in a car accident in the spring. I feel his discomfort as he offers his condolences. I quickly change the subject.

I wake up in a panic. We have ordered a new phone service and beginning the next day, our new service is to kick in. It suddenly dawns on me that Kristi's voice is on our answering machine.

"You've reached the Visocky's," her voice says. "We can't come to the phone right now. Please leave a message after the beep."

I call our home phone sometimes twenty times a day just to listen to her voice. Then I rush home from work to be there before Bob gets home so he will not see my number on the caller ID. He has a thing about always checking the phone to see who called. I don't want him to think I am losing my grip. With the change to the new service Kristi's voice will be gone.

"We have to cancel," I plead to Bob. "I can't lose her voice. It's all we have left."

"It might be too late for that," is his response. "Maybe there is someone who can save it or record it for us."

Bob calls a friend at the radio station who agrees to see what he can do. That evening his friend drops off a CD of Kristi's voice. The CD goes in my car and sometimes, as I drive, I play it over and over and I talk to her.

My days and weeks are filled with grief. I go to work every day, performing the duties that I must, wearing my mask to hide the pain that engulfs my body. At times I am not sure I can go on, but go on I must. Others have carried on, I guess I will also.

CHAPTER 4
I Will Survive

"Loss makes artists of us all as we weave new patterns in the fabric of our lives."
-Greta W. Cosby

We are nothing if not resilient. Life has a way of throwing challenges at us, pitching us into a fiery furnace of despair to be forged and molded and strengthened like tempered steel. Losing a loved one is one of the toughest tests of all, though there are others that can also wound us to the core.

I have been blessed with four beautiful children and each one holds a very special place in my heart, as does my husband, my parents, my siblings, and my grandchildren. When you lose someone, there is an empty space, and though your love for them lives on, there is a hole in your heart that feels as if it will never be filled.

How does one endure? By putting one foot in front of the other and by getting out of bed every day when all you want to do is pull the covers over your head. You stand straight, even when it feels as if you have been hit with a sucker punch square in the abdomen when not looking and you can hardly breathe. Or you just manage to find your way home after a day spent wandering the streets with a glazed look in your eyes, like a zombie void of all emotion, feeling only a deep angst in the pit of your stomach.

"You will survive this," others tell you.

"But I don't want to. I don't think I can," you say.

How *does* one survive the loss of a child? The heart is resilient, I am told, and I guess I have to believe that. Even when I lash out in anger at a universe that would take my child from me, I know that I will survive this. We women are especially good at resilience. Perhaps we have an extra gene that allows us to endure terrible loss, tragedy, and untold atrocities. We are, after all, a wondrous garden, first growing babies and then growing faith. Maybe all that sadness becomes a sort of compost, gradually breaking down to create fertile soil from which spring seeds of hope for a more beautiful, peaceful world.

My mother had resilience. She lived it in her own quiet way after losing her husband at age 38, raising five teenage children on her own, and still after being diagnosed with MS.

Bonnie has resilience, too, going to college at age 46 after her 17-year-old son Billy died. She is now a psychotherapist focusing on grief and loss, working with parents who have lost children.

Wendy has it. It is for her daughter Lacy who was brutally murdered that Wendy created the 2 Hearts 4 Lacy Foundation, dedicated to education, awareness, and prevention of violence. Wendy took her fierce determination to create something positive out of her daughter's death all the way to the Colorado State Legislature, spearheading the passage of Lacy's Law.

There's Beena, whose daughter Sonia died of cancer at the age of 17. Before her death, Sonia started a non-profit called Peace Is the Cure and boldly wrote a letter to then President Bush asking him to stop the war in Iraq for one day and dedicate the billions of dollars spent on the war towards cancer research. Even though still fighting her own battle with grief, Beena carries on her daughter's legacy, working to raise money for cancer research and promoting an end to war.

And Sarina, who after the death of her son J.T. realized she, too, was psychic, studied to become a gifted psychic medium. She now helps others connect with their loved ones on the other side.

It's amazing how many women I have come to know who have lost a child. This is not the place I envisioned my self, yet here I am, both unloading my grief and carrying another's, with a group of women that I never wanted to meet—strong women who share the load even when theirs is overwhelming.

Chapter 5

The Angel Reader

"The wings of angels are often found on the backs of the least likely people."
~ Eric Honeycutt

Amy calls early in the morning, as I am getting ready for work. A good friend of my son's, her brother died a couple years prior. She, too, is connected to this God damned club.

"You should go to a Compassionate Friends meeting," she tells me. "It's a support group for parents who have lost children. My mom goes regularly and it has been a big help to her. There's a meeting tonight. I'll go with you," she promises.

"Ok. I'll think about it." At least, that will end this conversation.

Amy calls back later that afternoon. She has a sick child and needs to go directly home after work. She won't be able to make the meeting. "But my mom will be there," she says. "Watch for her, she will help you."

Fuck that, I think. *I'm not going to go. I don't belong there.*

Attending would be confirmation that I am part of her club, a club I do not want to join. The required dues are high and once you are in, you can never leave. I am angry at her suggestion and for a while I try to pretend this club is not for me. But there is no denying it, I am an honorary member. The meeting is just a few blocks from my office and I have nowhere else to go. My husband is not expecting me home early. I know he is already on his way to his preferred coping place, the neighborhood pub. He can drink his sorrow away, or at least bury it for a little while.

I head over early and park across the street. I am chain smoking, another thing I do a lot lately, and am reluctant to get out of the car. *This is not for me, I can't do this.* I clutch the door handle but can't make myself open the door. *Perhaps I will just drive around for an hour.* It is then that I notice the other car. It is parked around the corner—a lone woman in the driver's seat. She has been there almost as long as I have. *What is she waiting for?* And then, there she is, walking down the sidewalk toward the door. I recognize the look in her eyes—the one of quiet desperation that I see in my mirror every day. I get out and approach her.

"I lost my daughter," I say.

"I lost my son," she responds.

We hold hands and walk in together.

There are about twenty people, men and women, all with that same desperate look. I am introduced to a woman who acts as the greeter. She asks me my name and who I have lost. I tell her my daughter died in a car accident a few weeks ago.

"Fresh grief," she says. "I'm so sorry."

That term sticks with me. *Fresh grief. As opposed to what? Stale grief or old grief?* I guess it makes sense. I think of fresh meat and realize I am raw with emotion.

We sit in a large circle, the leader of the group instructing us on how the meeting works. I think she must have the old grief variety, for she handles the rocky emotions of the group with ease and grace. We go around the room and share the name of our children, when and how they died and how old they were. It is horrible to sit in the circle and listen to everyone's story. Some have lost an older child like my daughter. Some have lost a baby. For some their child was still-born and there is one woman who is 70 years old; her daughter was 48 when she died. I realize a mother's pain is still the same, no matter the age; we are all crying. By the time it is my turn, I am certain I can't go through with it, but I am encouraged to talk about my daughter so I tell my story.

There is something unnerving about putting a bunch of grief-stricken parents together in the same room. I have a bizarre attraction to these people, all strangers, yet I realize they are my people now. I recoil at the thought.

This is the place where you learn that the thoughts in your head are not crazy. You can say things in this group that you can't tell anyone else. Things like:

"I almost stepped in front of a bus yesterday; it was all I could do to restrain myself."

"My daughter's voice is on our answering machine. I call home several times a day just to hear it. Then I rush home after work so I can clear the machine before my husband comes home."

"At night, I hug my daughter's ashes, rocking back and forth just as I did when she was a baby. I sing to her through my tears."

Tears flow openly at this meeting—no pretense, no need to be strong. Kleenex boxes are scattered around the circle and are gently shared.

I sit with the woman I walked in with. We are still holding hands. Her name is Joyce and I learn that her son Tyler died in a car accident just a couple months before Kristi. There are several parents of young people around the same age as Kristi in this group. *What is it with these kids that they would leave us so early?* One is forever changed by the loss of a loved one, especially a child. We like to think parents are not supposed to outlive their children, but we all know it is a lie.

My life is changed at this meeting. Not by the stories of the parents in this unspeakable club, or by connecting with other people who share something so tragic, but by one woman.

"Your daughter was standing behind you all night long, she's a beautiful girl," the woman says to me. I remember her from the circle. She hands me her card: Angel Reader.

What's an Angel Reader? What am I supposed to do with this? A psychic? Me talk to a psychic? I don't even know what they do. All I've seen are those gals on TV, you know, 1-800-PSYCHIC. This is too weird. I put the card in my pocket.

Chapter 6

We Agreed to Do This

"Is willing to accept that she creates her own reality except for some of the parts where she can't help but wonder what the hell she was thinking."
~ Brian Andreas

Three weeks have gone by since the encounter with the Angel Reader. The card sits on my desk, taunting me, whispering its secrets. This is your chance, it seems to say. *This is crazy*, I think. *Talk to a psychic? No way! But she can see Kristi; maybe she can talk to her.* I grab the card and dial the number.

I ring the doorbell with trepidation. *What am I doing?* In my heart, I know that I would do anything to be able to connect with my daughter again. I miss her so much.

Kristi used to call me every day at work. "Hey, what are you doing?" she'd ask when I answered the phone. Sometimes I would be impatient with her. I was busy working, and she always had so much to say. Out of four kids, Kristi was the talkative one. She always had something to share with me—every little detail, drama and event that was going on in her life. Too much information, I would complain, but now I would give anything to hear from her again.

The woman takes me to a quiet space in her home; the lights are dim and soft music is playing. She lights several candles and invites me to sit on the couch.

"Are you comfortable?" she asks.

"Yes," I say, even though comfortable is the last thing I am. *I don't even believe in this!*

She tells me she has had the gift of connecting with those from the other side since she was a child, but just really started to develop it over the last few years. She begins by saying a little prayer, asking her guides and angels to come in and help her connect.

"I see your daughter standing next to you. She has long blond hair."

"How do I know this is Kristi?" I ask.

She tells me several things about Kristi, things she couldn't possibly know.

"She has a tattoo, a dolphin, on her shoulder."

I am beginning to believe.

She describes the accident, feeling the impact on her left side and her head.

"Kristi was watching the result of the accident and then she came to you. She was with you when the chaplain came to the door and at the funeral. She wants you to know that she loves you and she is sorry it had to happen like this."

"If things had been different, would the outcome have been different?" I ask.

"How she died might have been different," Kristi responds through the woman, "but the outcome would have been the same. It was meant to be. We agreed to do this. And it has more to do with your soul's evolution than mine."

Great, I agreed to this pain. What the fuck was I thinking?

She talks about Kristi sending us signs: butterflies and pennies. I don't remember seeing any butterflies, but I vow to keep my eyes open.

I am excited to share my reading with Bob. He is skeptical, to say the least, about all this psychic stuff, but when I mention that Kristi sends us signs like butterflies, his face lights up. That very afternoon, while I was at the woman's he had gone golfing. He tells me that a yellow butterfly was following him around the golf course all afternoon, almost in his face, darting in and out with each stroke. He played one of the best games of his life. I see the glimmer of hope in his eyes; I hear the whisper of awe in his voice. He, too, wants to believe.

Given a book by Doreen Virtue about connecting with angels, I am soon scouring the Spirituality section at Barnes and Noble, reading anything I can find on angels and connecting to the other side. I read all the how-to-talk-to-dead-people books by authors such as Sylvia Browne, James Van Praagh, and others. I am amazed and excited to learn that our loved ones who have died can connect with us—try to connect, in fact—to let us know that they are fine and that they love us.

I learn that our loved ones reach out to us in many ways to let us know they are around. They may place common objects such as coins or a feather in our path, often in places they should not be. We may sense odors such as a loved one's favorite perfume or if the person was a smoker, cigarette or cigar smoke, wafting out of nowhere. Number sequences like their birth date or other relevant numbers may appear repeatedly on clocks, license plates, and billboards. We may hear a buzzing noise in our ears when our loved ones are trying to get our attention since they speak to us on a different, higher frequency. And Spirits love to play with electricity, often causing lights to flicker or electronic devices to turn on and off.

I am fascinated by all that I am discovering and though much of it is contrary to all that I thought I knew, in some weird way it is starting to make sense. *Why haven't I heard of this before? Perhaps because I didn't need it yet?*

I start to recognize the little signs and clues I feel are from Kristi. A butterfly, a particular song I know she loved on the radio just when I am thinking of her, strange things happening with our electronics.

I am in my office. It is an old building and can be kind of creepy if you are there alone. My secretary and I are the only ones in the place. We hear a crash and get up to investigate. We have a small kitchen area with a set of open shelves where we store plates, glasses, and coffee cups. We discover that a plate has not just fallen off the shelf but was literally thrown off the shelf, landing a good 5-6 feet away. It lies shattered on the floor. Is it Kristi just practicing her new-found abilities or the ghost who is known to inhabit our building? I don't know, but I am starting to believe that there are spirits around us, even if we can't see them.

I am dreaming . . . *I walk in my front door. It is our old house, the one my kids grew up in. Stairs are to the right, living room to the left. There is someone lying on the couch. Oh my God, it's Kristi! I rush to hug her.*

"Kristi, what are you doing here? How did you get here?"

"I don't know mom, but I can walk."

I hold her.

It is one of those dreams you don't want to leave. I try to hang on for as long as possible. *Please, please, don't let this end.* I wake up and Kristi is gone. According to the books I have been devouring, dreams are an easy way for spirits to connect with us. Our defenses are down and we are more receptive. I pray every night for Kristi to visit me again.

At times I think I can hear Kristi talking to me, but to be honest, I am not yet convinced that it is her. Perhaps it is just my imagination, fueled by the hunger to connect with her myself. *I'm trying, Kristi. I want to talk to you, to hear from you.*

Our daughter Jenny comes to us to tell us she is pregnant. A baby, how wonderful; that might fill the hole in our hearts. A few weeks later, while having a reading from a medium at the local holistic fair I am given a new message.

"Kristi has a little girl with her," the woman declares.

We know this baby is going to be a girl. When Hampton, our granddaughter is born, we recognize the small birthmark on her right thigh. It is the exact size, shape, and location as the one Kristi had; we know she is sent to us as a gift from Kristi to ease our pain.

Jenny was the last family member to see Kristi before she died. Kristi had stopped in at the restaurant where Jenny was tending bar. She had just finished work and was heading out to a dance club with friends. The two of them had recently reconciled, having not gotten along for the past several years. Four years apart with two very different personalities, each one sure the other was the favored child. Jenny once told me how strange it was as Kristi got up to leave. She gave Jenny a long hug and then turned to look back at her as she walked out the door. In retrospect, Jenny feels now that Kristi was saying goodbye.

It's funny how we are affected by death. Jenny had worked in the restaurant and bar business for years, but after Kristi's death she could not stomach it any more. She took time off for the funeral and never went back.

Chapter 7

Not the Same Person Any More

"If you think that things are different, it doesn't mean they have changed. Perhaps you have."
- Unknown

I am not the same person any more. Kristi's death has forever changed me. I am becoming more and more interested in this woo-woo stuff (my favorite term for spirituality-seeking), fascinated by such topics as spirituality, angels, psychic abilities, metaphysics, the meaning of life, God. I think I can spend the rest of my days reading books on angels, connecting to the other side, life after death. I used to love my job, helping to bring beautiful music to the world. Now I am consumed with exploring my newfound spirituality.

Weekends are spent wandering the aisles of the New Age section at Barnes and Noble. I grab a stack of books and park myself in one of the comfy reading chairs and am engrossed for hours.

One Saturday, *Conversations with God* by Neale Donald Walsch jumps off the shelf at me. I need to read this one for sure. I have had a few of my own conversations with God, all be it one-sided and more of a ranting on my part. I can't wait to see what God has to say. I challenge him to show me how all this makes sense. According to Walsch we are all a divine spark of God, here to experience life so that God, in turn, can come to know life and experience it through us. Interesting perspective and I sort of get it, though I question why in the world God would want to experience such grief and pain.

This book really gets me thinking. I re-evaluate all that I have been taught over the years. Traditional religion as I knew it now seems so restrictive, even down right wrong in many cases. It has surely done a number on my husband. The many phases of grief, the denial, the whys, etc., are tough enough, but for Bob there is an additional burden. Based on his Catholic upbringing, he struggles with the fact that Kristi had never been confirmed and because of that, she wouldn't go to heaven.

Now that's a bit much for me. I imagine Kristi standing in front of St. Peter at the proverbial pearly gates.

"Let's see," St. Peter says. "In kindergarten you were sent to the principal's office when you pushed a bigger boy on the playground for picking on Tommy, the handicapped child. And here you are in 9th grade, comforting a friend who just lost her mother." And with a chuckle, "Oh yes, there was that party hosted by the football team your freshman year at college. You really got in that guy's face when he wouldn't let the not-so-cool kids in. You told him that if those kids weren't good enough for his party, then you weren't either. And you left. I like that!"

But then St. Peter turns to Kristi with a frown, "Wait a minute. It says here that you were never confirmed. Sorry, I just can't let you into heaven. It's one of our rules." And St. Peter sends her away.

For my husband who had these ideas drilled into his head from the time he was a small child, it is difficult to set them aside. For me, coming from a different experience growing up, it makes me angry. Who made up all these rules anyway? What's the purpose of discounting the contributions of a good life because of something so trivial? And whatever happened to all the Catholics who went to Hell for eating meat on Friday?

I have long struggled with the viewpoint of many traditional religions. I find it exasperating that each one proclaims to believe in God, a God so powerful that He created the entire Universe, yet still these religions have the audacity to declare that only those who believe exactly as they do are going to be saved; the rest of us are all going to Hell. It didn't make sense to me before and makes even less sense now, the notion that a God who is able to create such a vast and diverse Universe would only provide us with one path Home.

When my husband and I got married, we had to meet with my Lutheran minister for pre-marriage instruction. He asked me if I agreed that if one didn't believe in Jesus Christ then that person wouldn't go to heaven. I, in turn, asked him about a person growing up in India who was raised Hindu. "What if he never had a chance to learn about Jesus yet led an exemplary life; does that mean he would go to Hell?" Let's just say he wasn't very pleased with me. I truly believe there are many paths to God. To me it is more about how we live our life than what dogma we choose to follow.

I am beginning to see the fallacy in the Western world's take on dying. Too often we are taught that this one life is all there is and when it ends, that's it. Or, instead of once again returning to a loving God who welcomes us back Home with open arms, we are told that when we die we must stand in front of a stern and unforgiving deity who sits on a throne and looks at every mistake we have ever made, deciding if we are good enough to enter heaven. And, if we do make it past that stringent test, we certainly aren't able to visit our friends and family still living. No wonder so many of us are afraid of death.

I also find it fascinating that most religions believe in angels or wise ascended souls who brought messages to certain people on earth (Moses and Noah, for example) thousands of years ago, but deny that such an occurrence can happen now. *What, did God just decide not to talk to us anymore?*

The New Age section at the bookstore has many offerings, a vast and tantalizing smorgasbord of topics to choose from: spirituality, psychic phenomenon, past lives and more. I devour them fervently, like a starving man, hungry for nourishment. I gorge as if my life depends on it. Perhaps it does.

The Four Agreements, a simple yet profound book by don Miguel Ruiz, touches my soul. Written with gentleness and heart, it is based on four tenants: (1) Be Impeccable with Your Word, (2) Don't Take Anything Personally, (3) Don't Make Assumptions, and (4) Always Do Your Best. Life should be simple, I think. How do we manage to complicate it so?

Many Lives, Many Masters by Brian Weiss, M.D. somehow finds its way to my growing stack of books. Weiss describes our relationship with past lives as we follow his journey from Head of Psychiatry at Mount Sinai Medical Center, Miami to believer and teacher of reincarnation. According to Weiss, the earth plane is a school and to further our soul's evolution we incarnate again and again to have new experiences, fresh opportunities to expand our awareness. A psychic medium once told me that Kristi and I had shared many lives together. It is starting to make sense.

Hanging out one Saturday morning, I notice a woman also perusing the New Age section. I ask her what books she might recommend and she, in turn, asks me if I have heard of Abraham-Hicks. She tells me about Abraham, a group consciousness from the non-physical dimension, channeled by a woman by the name of Esther Hicks. This is interesting. I have never really heard of channeling before. Grabbing a cup of coffee, we visit for over an hour as she introduces me to the concept of channeling, the act or practice of serving as a medium through which a spirit guide purportedly communicates with living persons. *Who knew something like that was even possible?* She goes on to describe the Law of Attraction, the belief that we are all energy and that our thoughts and words act as a giant transmitter/receiver—what we send out, we get back. As she gets up to leave she hands me an Abraham-Hicks CD.

"I think you'll enjoy this," she says. "Best of luck on your journey."

Plugging the CD into my car stereo, I listen to the voice of Abraham-Hicks intently as I drive around town, unable to return to my empty house, fascinated by this new perspective. According to Abraham, we are the creators of our reality, as opposed to some outside force, fate or happenstance. It is a concept I struggle with. I am not sure if I want to be in charge of my life. The thought is both daunting and exciting at the same time. I begin analyzing the energy that I am sending out. *What am I creating?*

I read books by Deepak Chopra, Marianne Williamson, Alan Cohen, Wayne Dyer and others. The stack next to my bed is growing taller by the week. So much astonishing information, why is it I did not know about this before? A whole new world is revealed to me. *These are the answers I have been looking for.* All those questions, some I didn't even know I had, are being answered.

I liken it to sitting in a very dim room. We have been in this room for quite some time and are very confident in what we know about it, in fact, we are pretty sure we know everything in the room: the sofa, the chair, the little side table. The room is simple, small and four-sided like a box. We have grown comfortable with it, having resided in this space for as long as we can remember.

Then one day someone turns on the light and suddenly we see the beautiful paintings on the walls, the intricate crown molding bordering the ceiling, the coat rack in the corner, a book shelf filled with many volumes, a green plant and interesting memorabilia, items we never realized were there. Where did this all come from? We wonder in awe as we survey the space noticing first one thing then another, discovering little nooks and crannies filled with even more. We're pretty sure these weren't here before, and if they were, why could we not see them?

We learned in school, oh so many years ago, that we have five senses: sight, sound, touch, taste, and smell. We have accepted as truth the view that the world consists of only that which can be detected by the five senses. As difficult as it might be to believe, I begin to realize there is a vast universe surrounding us, countless dimensions beyond those our senses can detect. It is a quantum field filled with other realities just waiting to be discovered by us. I am ready to step into the light. I want to know more. I want to understand.

"Kristi came to me this morning. She has a message for you."

The email lands in my in box without fanfare. It comes from a woman I had just met a week ago. Kimmie Rose Zapf is a psychic medium from Michigan. We met at a book event in Denver and immediately hit it off. I am surprised to hear from her and especially to hear that Kristi had visited her.

"She said she will meet you at the base of the mountain."

Kimmie goes on to describe the mountain, tall and lush and green with huge boulder outcrops. At the base is a river.

Where is this mountain? What do you want me to do? I can't imagine where the mountain might be, but I will do anything to find it. I want to meet you there. My heart is breaking, I so long to connect with you. Please show me where it is, Kristi.

It has been two years since you left us Kristi. Why are you sending me this message now?

CHAPTER 8

Nothing to Lose

"How do geese know when to fly to the sun?
Who tells them the seasons?
How do we humans know when it is time to move on?
As with the migrant birds,
so surely with us, there is a voice within
if only we would listen to it,
that tells us certainly when to go for the unknown."
~ Elisabeth Kubler-Ross

Take ten deep breaths and ask the angels what it is you need to know today.

A friend had shared this technique with me and I practice it steadfastly for a week with no results. I want to be able to connect to my angels, the guides that these books and teachers are saying we all have, but so far I have not gotten any messages from angels or anyone else. It feels hopeless; maybe I don't have this gift or maybe I don't have any guardian angels who want to talk with me.

I begin breathing slowly, deeply, counting as I go. 1, 2, 3 . . .

"Quit your job." The voice is loud and clear in my head as I mentally tally breath number 10.

"What?" I ask.

"Quit your job." I hear the command again. *Great, I finally get a message and it's telling me to quit my job. How do I explain that to my boss? My husband, my family, my friends?* I am hearing voices in my head and they are telling me to quit my job. My family already thinks I'm crazy.

I'm not sure what I am supposed to do with this information, but in my heart I know the answer. My path has been laid out for me, one that began when my daughter died. There is no turning back.

Sometimes we start out in life heading down a particular path and we think that is who we are and what we do. Then along comes something that sends us spiraling in a completely different and often unknown direction. It is frightening, taking the leap into the unfamiliar; consequently we wrestle with our choices, going back and forth between one and the other, immobilized, unable to move. But sooner or later comes a time in everyone's life when we can no longer ride the fence. We reach a choice point and it is time to act. For many of us, we talk about the day we are going to do this or that, we envision, we plan, we dream. But too often we fail to take the leap to that which is calling us. We are afraid to step out of our comfort zone, or the security of what we have, even if we don't like it. We justify our reluctance to change by listing all the responsibilities we have and the expectations of others, or maybe, which is true of me, we don't value ourselves, our gifts and even our contribution. We've all heard the expression, "Do what you love and the money will follow." Really? We all know plenty of starving artists; it doesn't sound like they've figured out the *do what you love* thing.

How do we take the leap, especially when nothing about the move makes sense? How do we grasp what our heart is telling us? The body knows; our intuition, that gut feeling we get, is our director and understands what our soul wants. When we pay attention we have access to all the information we need to guide our lives. Best-selling author Alan Cohen suggests that we flip a coin. If its heads we will do a specific thing, tails we will not. What's interesting, though, it's not the face of the coin that gives us our answer, it's the feeling we get when we see what side is up. Did it make you happy, or did you sigh and think, *damn, that's not what I wanted*? That's our intuition talking and it always knows what's best for us.

Two years after my daughter died I was at such a choice point. While I enjoyed the organization I worked for, I realized my passion for my job was waning. I was consumed by my new spiritual path and my search for answers. I wanted to learn more. I wanted to be able to see and hear these visionaries who fed my soul through their books. Someone needed to bring them to my city. Gradually it dawned on me—that someone was me. I looked back on my life, at the many successful events and programs I had coordinated for the symphony and other organizations, everything from concerts, fundraisers, and citywide festivals, to hockey and golf tournaments—so many things over the years it almost made my head spin. Was it training perhaps for what I was thinking about now? Was I to apply all that I had learned to my new passion?

It was time for me to take the leap.

After all, what have I got to lose? I've already lost my daughter, if I lose my house, it's just a house.

I felt as if I had found my purpose. I was to produce events with these new thought speakers I had been discovering. Surely if I was interested in their message others would be as well. I hoped, just maybe, they would want to take this journey with me. I was going to ignite the world, or at least Fort Collins.

Once I made my decision, I needed a name for my business. The tagline came first, Igniting Change. Next we needed a spark. That's it—something spark! One Spark, Two Spark, Red Spark, Blue Spark. I went through the list, trying on names; nothing quite having the impact I was looking for. It had to be perfect. I was in the shower when it came to me—BellaSpark (Some of my best ideas come when in the shower—something about the water being a great conductor of energy, I guess.). Bella means beautiful in Italian and Kristi definitely was a beautiful spark. She was the catalyst for me to begin this journey; it is only fitting that she be the inspiration for its name. BellaSpark it is.

With an empty credit card in my pocket and a fire in my belly, I got up the courage to produce my first event. Sonia Choquette, author of *Trust Your Vibes*, agreed to speak in Fort Collins; thank you Sonia for trusting me. Nervously I prepared, taking advantage of all my past skills and then some. And though I had considerable experience when it came to organizing events, this time it was different. This time it was for me.

As it turned out there were plenty of other people who, like me, were searching for answers. They came in droves, 500 of them to be exact, all delighted that someone of this caliber was coming to Fort Collins. I could almost feel the vibration of the hall rise.

Convinced that I had chosen the right path, encouraged that Spirit was guiding me, I was ready to take the next step. I drew on my experience gained from producing concert series for the symphony. What if there was a series of new thought speakers? If 500 people liked one speaker, they would surely like five. I called it The Extraordinary People Series, featuring many of the world's leading visionaries, seers, and teachers. I invited the teachers that had inspired me: Neale Donald Walsch, of course; Doreen Virtue with her angel messages; psychic mediums such as James Van Praagh and John Holland who brought comfort and solace to people who have lost a loved one; Brian Weiss exploring past lives; also don Miguel Ruiz, Alan Cohen, and so many more. Authors and speakers with powerful messages; there was an overwhelming desire to learn from them, to know them personally, to understand how and why they did what they did. Perhaps they could show me the way.

I signed a contract with our largest performance hall for five nights. At 1200 seats it is a big space. *What am I thinking? Are there really that many people in this area who think like me? Who are searching for answers? Who are saying, "There has to be more than this"?* I crossed my fingers and prayed.

For many of us it is difficult to take big risks. We want a guarantee; we want to be sure each move we make is the right one. However, sooner or later, we all learn there are no guarantees in life. And often it is a dark night of the soul that forces us out of our comfort zone and propels us toward something else. My dark night of the soul was Kristi's death. It's hard to believe that there is a purpose and Divine plan for things when we are hurting and in the depths of despair; letting go of our fear is not easy. It is only when we accept that God/Spirit is always with us and there is a much bigger or different plan for us, a perfect plan, that we find the courage to take the leap. After all, what have we got to lose?

A woman approached me about purchasing her business, *The Healing Path* magazine. She had been publishing the magazine for thirteen years; time to pass it off to someone new. I said yes. *What do I know about running a magazine?* Not much, but I couldn't shake the feeling that I was being divinely guided. The name was telling; I was, after all, on my own healing path.

We took out a second mortgage on our home. While signing the papers I did not experience the typical buyer's remorse. This was one of the few decisions in my life I did not question. Bob agreed to handle the advertising side of the business, my daughter Jenny came on board as office manager, and I was guided to a woman, Linda Potter, who took on the job of editor. An accomplished writer, she was as passionate about planting spiritual seeds as I was. Together we created *BellaSpark Magazine*, hoping to be the spark and ignite change for those who, like us, were searching for answers.

My new life was taking shape and it was nothing I could have ever planned. All I could do was trust that I was on the right path.

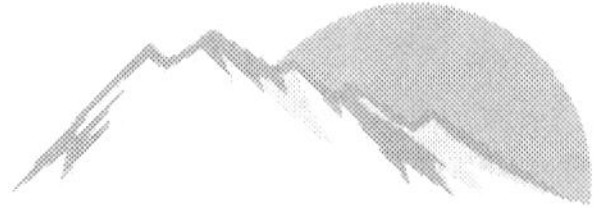

CHAPTER 9
Do You Believe in Angels?

"When angels visit us, we do not
hear the rustle of wings,
nor feel the feathery touch of
the breast of a dove;
but we know their presence
by the love they create in our hearts."
~ Unknown

The Extraordinary Speaker Series is coming together. The first event kicks off in January. I have been working diligently to bring all the pieces together. Today I decide I deserve a break. I head out on my bike for a long ride. It is a beautiful fall day, my favorite time of year. There is something about the sound of the wind rustling the trees with their brittle leaves, the brilliant colors, red, gold, and orange and the coolness in the mornings that feed my soul as I ride along the wooded trails in Fort Collins. The fallen leaves make a crunching sound under my wheels as I roll over them. I always receive a lot of inspiration when I am on my bike, especially riding through the countryside. It's my way of meditating, finding a freedom and tranquility I can't find at home.

Thoughts of my upcoming speaker series are tumbling though my head, freely flowing in and out like the breeze. I visualize the speakers taking the stage, imagine what it would be like to meet them, and fantasize about who else I would like to work with. I think of Deepak Chopra and imagine what it would be like to bring him to Fort Collins one day. So far, I haven't been able to connect with his office, but some day, I vow, Deepak Chopra will also be one of my speakers. Not only will it be amazing to have him in my home town, but more than anything I want to meet this man who has been at the forefront of new thought for many years. I envision him in the lineup along with others who inspire me.

I can't pick up Deepak Chopra in Bob's Buick! The thought hits me like a ton of bricks.

I need a limo to drive my speakers. I need a limo company to come on board as a sponsor and pick my speakers up at the airport. How do I do that? I don't know any limo companies.

I have been reading Doreen Virtue's books for some time now. She talks about how to connect with your angels and how anyone can ask them for help with things. I figure maybe I should ask my angels to bring me a limo company. It's worth a shot. I send my request out to the angels and promptly forget about it as I head home to get ready for an evening out with my husband. We've been invited to the grand opening of a new hotel; should be a nice time. Lots of good food and wine, interesting people; I love those kinds of parties.

The evening has been great fun. Bob and I would separate and socialize, come together, and then split up again to see who else we knew. It's been delightful, but I think the wine is going to my head and I am ready to call it a night as I wander about looking for my husband.

"He's over there talking to some limo lady," a friend directs me.

I had not mentioned to Bob my thoughts about finding a limo company to sponsor my events, but sure enough, there he is talking to a woman he knows from somewhere, and yes, she does own a limo company. Joining their conversation, I figure what the heck; I might as well see what she thinks. I tell her a little bit about BellaSpark Productions and my vision for the upcoming Extraordinary People Series and the speakers I'm planning on bringing to Fort Collins. Not only has she heard of people like Deepak Chopra and Doreen Virtue, but she loves them! She practically begs me to let her drive my speakers.

I walk away in awe. *Wow. That was really fast. 9:00 in the morning to 9:00 at night. These angels really know how to get things done!*

I have come to believe we all have angels, guides, and loving souls who are with us all the time. They help steer us on our soul's path, regularly sending us signs and messages. Our job is to open our eyes and listen. The idea of a group of angels surrounding me reminds me of an old television commercial for Verizon Wireless. This guy comes out of the store after purchasing Verizon phone service and is greeted by hundreds of people lead by a man in a grey uniform. As he walks, the man in the grey uniform and the throng of people move with him. Every step he takes, the crowd shifts to follow him, two steps to the left, three steps to the right; they all move as one with him. Bewildered, the man goes back inside the store and asks, "What's up?"

"It's your network," is the reply.

I like to imagine that we, too, have such a network, only ours is made up of our angels and guides, there to help us day in and day out. They follow us wherever we may go, every step we take, every move we make (Hmmm, sounds like a song!). They give us assistance as we go through our day. I will visualize literary angels when I am writing. I call on my speaking angels when I am about to address a group of people. There are business angels guiding me as I navigate the ins and outs of publishing and artist angels who help me when I need to be creative. My favorites are the finding angels who help me locate my cell phone and car keys, and the parking angels really come in handy. Sometimes, all we have to do is ask.

I am slowly discovering my own guides and angels. One by one they make themselves known to me. My favorite guide says his name is David. How do I know? A book I have been studying encourages readers to ask our guides what we want to know, questions like: Who are you? What's your name? Why are you with me? So I asked him. David's a little goofy looking—sort of reminds me of Lyle Lovett—and he always has a smile on his face. Whenever I think of him or feel him near I smile. I am smiling now as I write about this. One morning while out riding my bike, I carried on a conversation with David. Looking for confirmation that I was not making this up, I asked for a sign from him. *If you're really with me, then the next bike that comes down this path will be red.* Sure enough, the next bike to come around the bend was bright red. Why was I not surprised? When I asked what his duty was, the voice in my head responded "I am your muse." I liked that.

I am also getting to know Zura, tall and dark like an African queen, and Jesus, who I feel continues to guide me as he has since

I was a child. I learn I have a big blue angel that is always with me.

I have a friend who once said he didn't think there was anyone out there; no God or angels were helping him. How lonely that must be. I would much rather believe that we are each surrounded by our own network that we can call on for help, that we are connected to all the knowledge of the Universe whenever we need it. We just need to ask and then be open to the answer.

Chapter 10
Me, Psychic?

"Everyone is psychic.
Being psychic is not a particular talent.
Everybody has a left foot.
Some people may just walk with that foot,
some people may drag it,
and some may learn to dance with it."
- Dr. Frederick Lenz

Now that I have awakened to this woo-woo stuff I am increasingly more and more aware of the psychics, mediums, healers, and various practitioners in our community—amazing that I couldn't see them before. I guess they were there all the time, just not on my radar. I learn there are classes for people who want to become more psychic. These classes aren't only for those who want to do readings for others, connecting them to their loved ones who have passed on. They also have much to offer those who just want to connect on their own without going through a medium.

I have met many psychic mediums who can remember having a sixth sense as a child but quickly learned to shut it down or hide it, discouraged by well-meaning parents who either didn't understand or were afraid of their powers. It wasn't until later in life, often after a traumatic experience that their psychic aptitude returned. These gifts were not just passed out to certain people, though many have a heightened awareness. We, too, were given those abilities when we came to this earth plane, as my grandchildren can attest. We just lost them along the way.

How does one learn to connect with their guides, angels, and past loved ones? For someone like me, who long ago was taught that angels and imaginary friends don't exist, that when people die they just go away, it takes a little work. Actually sometimes it takes a lot of work, depending on how deep one's beliefs and walls are. The good news is we can recover our gifts with a little practice, if we want to. I use the term recover because in actuality, the capabilities are still there; we have just forgotten them. There are many tools to develop our psychic abilities, and just like any talent—whether it's golfing, speaking a foreign language, or cooking—it takes desire and practice to get better at it.

I have been visiting psychics and mediums for over two years now, ever since Kristi died. It is time I figure out how to do this myself. I am determined to learn how to increase my intuitive skills. I have no interest in being a psychic medium, talking to other people's dead people. If I can connect to my daughter and my guides, maybe my parents, I will be happy. I figure that if we all have latent psychic abilities, maybe there is a smattering of memory buried in the recesses of my mind. I sign up for a class on building your psychic tool kit; I'm determined to give it a try.

There are about fifteen of us curious souls in the class, all wondering if we, too, have the same talents as the psychics we go to for answers at the local holistic fair. The instructor, the same angel reader who first connected me with Kristi, introduces us to a list of claires (clair, from the French word meaning clear): Clairvoyance—clear seeing, Clairaudience—clear hearing, Clairsentience—clear feeling, Claircognizance—clear knowing. All of these mean that one has the ability to experience beyond the range of ordinary perception. Not only do we all have these abilities, albeit shut down in many of us, but it turns out we also have a *dominant clair*, one that is much easier for us to access. *I wonder what my dominant clair is?*

I also learn that because we are all energy, everything vibrates at a certain level. Obviously since we live in a physical plane our vibration is much lower than that of a being in a higher realm. In order to connect and communicate we must learn to raise our vibration while at the same time the spirits on the other side must lower theirs. When we are able to match our frequencies, much like tuning an FM radio dial, voila, the music happens!

We are given a list of tools to help us sharpen our skills. Finally, by mid-afternoon, the time comes for us to practice what we have learned. We are divided into two groups, each with an accomplished psychic medium to lead us. One person is chosen as the receiver, and we are told to focus on her, to try to tune in and see what kind of messages we might get. I have never thought of myself as intuitive. *What if I don't see, hear, or notice anything? What if everyone else gets clear communication and I talk about something that doesn't make any sense to this woman?*

At first I see nothing. Maybe I am trying too hard. *Wait, is that a windmill I see in my mind's eye?* It looks like something from

Hans Christian Andersen, the kind you see in Holland. And there is the little Dutch boy with his finger in the dike. *This is pretty cool, but what does it have to do with this woman I am supposed to be focusing on?*

"I want to speak to my wife!" The voice in my head comes out of nowhere and obliterates the vision I am just starting to enjoy.

"What?" I ask, thinking the words rather than speaking them out loud.

"I want to speak to my wife!" The man/voice is more persistent this time.

"I don't know how to do this," I respond.

"Yes you do. I want to speak to my wife!" the voice snaps at me.

Thankfully my message from the unseen realms is cut short as our leader brings the group back together again. I am noticeably rattled—this is not the loving voice from the other side I expected to hear. We go around the circle, each taking a turn sharing what we experienced. The receiver confirms some of the information; other pieces do not seem to make sense to her. Finally, it is my turn. I am still a little unsettled and certainly do not trust anything I have encountered during the last several minutes. I guess I have to say something. I tell her about the windmills.

"Where are you from?" I ask.

"Holland," she replies.

Of course she is; one point for me. I get up the courage to ask if her husband had died.

"Yes, three years ago."

"What was he like?" I probe.

Her description of her husband is not at all like the voice who was just bellowing in my head. Kind, sophisticated, a scholar, and a gentleman—she has nothing but nice things to say about him.

"I must have connected with someone else. This man was nothing like that." I share the message I had gotten. She begins to laugh.

"Yes, my husband was a gentleman, unless you got in his way. When he wanted something and couldn't have it, look out! That sounds exactly like him."

Wow, maybe I am psychic after all.

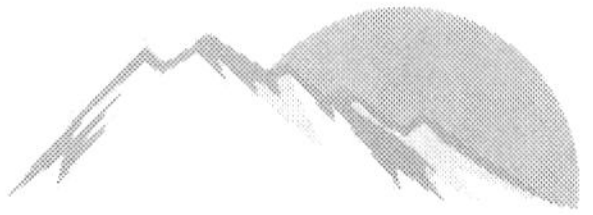

CHAPTER 11

Everyone Has a Story

"There is no greater agony than bearing an untold story inside you."
~ Maya Angelou

There are certain topics that are taboo. In polite conversation one never talks about money, except maybe to complain about not having enough. We certainly do not ask someone how much money they make, or share our own income. Religion and politics are also off limits, unless of course you are looking for a fight. Sexuality used to be on the list; remember the military's Don't Ask, Don't Tell policy? Thank goodness that one's been repealed. Spirituality, paranormal experiences and psychic phenomenon are other subjects that one never discusses; after all, people might think you are one of those woo-woo wackos who wear airy-fairy clothes, listen to psychics and plan your life around your astrological sign.

Some people find a passion and quietly go about their day, working on it individually, purposefully but singularly. I am not one of those people. When excited about something, or after having a life-changing experience, I want to share it with the world. Everyone should know about this; after all, this stuff is really cool. Who wouldn't want to be privy to such amazing information?

I am so excited to share my newfound experiences that I have to tell everyone and anyone who will listen. My friends and family sit patiently as I expound on my new obsession. Psychic readings, signs and messages from Kristi, this book, that speaker, weird and unexplainable happenings that come with exploring unseen realms; it is all I can talk about. At first, I feel they are patronizing me, listening out of pity. A funny thing happens though. The more I talk the more open they become. Soon, the stories we're sharing are theirs.

For you see, we all have them—stories and incidences that can't be explained, ghost tales, visits from loved ones who have passed on, messages from the other side and more. We know there is something else going on, something that cannot be explained in logical terms, but we lock it away and don't talk about it to anyone. After all, someone might think we're crazy.

Seems we are all in the closet, the psychic closet. It's fascinating; we share jokes and gossip and tales of sexual exploits, but weird phenomena or encounters with ghosts or angels we hide so deep we almost convince ourselves they never happened. Interestingly enough though, when we dare to open up to someone with our story, it's like a valve is unlocked and pretty soon their story comes pouring out, a gusher of emotion grateful to be released from its self-imposed prison. Sharing our story gives others permission to share theirs. Sometimes that's all we need, permission.

A Catholic School Boy's Story

We were in northern Wisconsin, an overdue visit to our hometown to attend my husband's class reunion. Bob grew up in this small town and attended Catholic school his entire young life. It gives you an idea of the barriers I sometimes faced with my husband who is still not quite ready to let go of the rules and dogma that were pounded into his head, often by a strict nun with a ruler.

At the reunion, while doing the usual meet and greet routine of catching up with old friends, wracking our brains trying to recognize people we hadn't seen in years, and wondering how they got to look so old, Carl, the husband of one of Bob's classmates asked me what I do. I told him I produce events for metaphysical speakers, folks like Wayne Dyer and Deepak Chopra. His blank look told me he'd never heard of these people. I said we also publish a magazine that features stories on holistic health, spirituality and even psychic mediums. With that his interest was piqued.

"You mean people like John Edward?' he asked.

"Yes, I have worked with several well-known mediums."

He proceeded to tell me his story.

Carl's friend Dave had passed away a few months prior. One day Dave showed up in Carl's house. Carl walked into the kitchen and Dave was there. A few days later, he showed up in the bedroom, then garage; seemed like every time Carl turned around, Dave was there. Carl could see him as plain as day. He tried talking to his wife, however, being a good Catholic girl, she would not even consider the thought that Dave might be reaching out to them. It was just wrong in her eyes. So Carl began watching the psychic John Edward on television at 4:00 a.m. just to wrap his arms around what he was experiencing.

What a relief it was to Carl to be able to share his story with me, someone who didn't think he was crazy. He asked me if I had any copies of my magazine. I gave him a copy, which he carefully folded in half, tucked in his back pocket and pulled his shirt down over the top so no one could see. Carl desperately wanted to share his story, but didn't feel comfortable until I gave him permission.

A Car Salesman's Story

I am always fascinated when I come across someone who doesn't fit the typical woo-woo mold, yet shares an interest in this spiritual information.

"My daughter lent me a book about past lives, *Many Lives, Many Masters*. It was so good I had to read it twice."

The comment came from a friend of ours as he described a book he had been reading to a co-worker. Both worked at a local car dealership. Bob and I were at the golf course, sitting on the patio having a beer with a group of friends. Mostly my husband's golfing buddies, it was an eclectic collection of car salesmen and bar patrons. Ruminating over their golf scores and grumbling about the dismal performance of the local baseball team were the typical topics of conversation. So to say I was shocked at their discussion was an understatement. I was even more surprised when the co-worker asked to borrow the book. These were car salesmen after all; you know the stereotype. Who'd have guessed they, of all people, would be interested in past lives? Seems spiritual seekers come in all shapes, sizes, and professions. I told our friend that the author, Brian Weiss, was going to be speaking in Fort Collins that fall and gave him a ticket to the lecture. He was thrilled and I was impressed that he had the confidence to share his interest.

Bob's Story

It is interesting that my husband, who doesn't trust any of this woo-woo stuff and is determined not to go down this path, has seen Kristi on more than one occasion. Bob is hesitant to admit it but he has actually seen her with his own two eyes. It is a fact that frustrates me to no end. While I connect with my daughter on many levels, I do not have the sight Bob does; I am jealous of his ability.

When our niece Dana got married and asked Bob to give her away, he reluctantly agreed. It was difficult for him. Much as he loved his niece, he was taking on a role he had envisioned he would have with his daughter. As the wedding processional began, Bob was standing at the back of the church with the bride-to-be behind the large center doors. As the doors opened, who did he see walking backwards down the aisle? None other than Kristi, giving him a big thumbs up.

"I told you I would be here Dad," she said smiling.

My Coming Out

I remember when I officially came out of the psychic closet. I was invited to be interviewed for a new magazine featuring community women and their journeys. Still serving in my role as Executive Director of the area's premier arts organization and an active participant in our community's thriving arts and cultural scene, I was delighted to be featured in their publication. However, though I loved the arts and what I did, I had become more and more interested in my newfound spiritual path, so much so that it was all I could talk about. My meeting with the magazine's writer started out pretty straightforward; however, soon I was once again sharing my stories about Kristi, the signs and messages she sent me. It's was a topic I loved to share and she seemed pretty interested, which merely fed my desire to impart this information even more.

It was only afterwards that I went into a panic. *How could I have said all those things?* I was, after all, a bit of a public figure in the community. *I work with businessmen and political figures; what will people think of me?* I even went so far as to call the magazine to see if I could review the article before it went to print. Sorry, I was told, not allowed. I was forced to wait three weeks until the magazine came out. *Is this the end of my professional career?*

It wasn't bad. Yes, I sounded a little woo-woo, but not totally crazy; I figured I could live with it. The reaction I received was surprising; people I thought I knew, and many people I didn't, told me how much they enjoyed what I had to say. And then, they shared their story, thanking me for giving them permission to reveal what they had been afraid to discuss with anyone else.

It is interesting to watch as we slowly come out of the psychic closet—the co-workers who bump into each other in the lobby during a BellaSpark event and realize all this time they shared an office and never knew the other was interested in this topic; the neighbors who pass each other, exchanging almost embarrassed looks that their secret is out. Why are we so afraid of this? What is it about believing that we are more than just this body, that we exist more than this lifetime, which forces us to close off this part of our knowing?

There are far too many of us in this closet. It *is* time we came out. Maybe we should have a giant coming-out party. Who knows who we might run into?

Three years have passed since Kristi left us. My life has gone in an entirely new direction since her death. I have learned much about what happens when we die and I truly believe that life does goes on and that our loved ones are near, but despite all I have come to know, my heart still aches for my daughter. Life is not the same without her.

Kimmie Rose is in Fort Collins. BellaSpark is hosting her event Messages from the Other Side. She is doing psychic readings for members of the audience, connecting them with loved ones who have passed. I am standing in the back secretly wishing she would call on me. "Pick me, pick me," my mind is saying, but I don't expect her to look at me. I don't usually get called on for a reading when I host an event; after all, the messages are for the paying guests.

"Donna, this one is for you. Kristi is here and she has a message for you."

I am stunned, and pleased.

"She says she will meet you at the base of the mountain."

Again she goes on to describe a big beautiful mountain, tall and lush and green with a river at the base.

I tell Kimmie she gave me the same message a year ago and I still don't know where the mountain is.

Come to me Kristi, I pray. Tell me where the mountain is. I am listening.

CHAPTER 12

Finding Stillness

"To understand the immeasurable,
the mind must be extraordinarily quiet, still."
~ Jiddu Krishnamurti

Every speaker I work with, every book I read, emphasizes the benefits of meditation as a means to connect with our higher self, with those who have once again returned to the God source of all energy, with Spirit itself. The Tibetan word for meditation, Gom, means to become familiar with one's Self.

For millennia, meditation has been a spiritual practice for serious seekers. By quieting the mind and deeply relaxing the body, the meditator experiences deep states of inner peace, and ultimately, higher states of awareness. There are many benefits to practicing meditation—stress relief, greater intuition, compassion, awareness, focus, among others—but they are secondary. Ultimately, meditation is the practice of seeking union with God.

By meditating you will develop the ability to see, feel, and hear more clearly. The more connected you are within yourself, the more you can connect with others. The more you can connect with others, the more you can achieve a sense of unity and oneness with your environment and the universe as a whole.

What is the difference between meditation and prayer? According to Suzanne Giesemann, author of *Messages of Hope*, prayer is asking, meditation is listening. While prayer may be the best way to talk to God, the key to listening to God is meditation.

Meditation is definitely one of the most effective ways to contact our loved ones on the other side. Clearing our thoughts and quieting the mind helps us to open the channels, to hear their voice or feel their presence. It is a skill and like any other skill it can be learned. It just takes practice and perseverance. Spending even ten to fifteen minutes a day meditating will make a profound difference in our ability to connect both with those who have passed and our guides and angels.

I am learning to meditate, to sit in silence, breathe deeply and slow the monkey mind chatter that constantly distracts me; the thoughts about what to make for dinner tonight, the work I need to finish up, the laundry I should attend to. I admit it is difficult at first. My brain just refuses to shut up. But countless spiritual gurus keep recommending it; there must be something to it. I am determined to get the hang of it.

We spend far too much time doing, tied up in the rat race we have created, and not enough time just being. Busyness has become our way of life; there is always more to do. Somewhere along the way we decided that if we weren't doing something or accomplishing something, we weren't valued. Or perhaps we are so uncomfortable with ourselves we fill the silence with numerous distractions such as television, noise, and chaos. Better to not know what our soul is trying to tell us, not feel the emotions welling up inside, begging to be heard.

It is in the quiet moments that Spirit speaks to us. I am practicing being quiet, first just ten minutes then gradually longer and longer. Once I reach that stillness within, I find that my guides and angels and yes, my loved ones, are able to break through the clutter and talk to me. I am open to receive the energies and messages. It is so delicious, so peaceful; I am content to stay there.

There are wonderful meditations available everywhere. Some are guided, others finely tuned music that can take you to that place of stillness. And meditation needn't only be sitting. I often find that inner peace while walking in the woods or riding my bike. Just being in nature, connecting with the natural world is an amazing way to reconnect with not only ourselves, but with Spirit, our guides, angels, and loved ones.

I try to meditate every day now, though I confess, it doesn't always happen. Meditation has become the best part of my day. I find that the day flows so much easier when I take the time to connect to Spirit. I am learning to ask questions, and yes, I do receive answers, guidance and support. I am also learning to trust my intuition, to listen to the gut feelings, my body's response when I have to make a decision, not quite sure which way to go. For I know it is my higher self talking to me. It is there that I find the answers I am searching for.

CHAPTER 13

Our Soul's Plan

"Character cannot be developed in ease and quiet.
Only through experience of trial
and suffering can the soul
be strengthened, ambition inspired,
and success achieved."
- Helen Keller

In the fascinating book *Your Soul's Plan*, Robert Schwartz asks the question: When something devastating happens to us, such as losing a loved one or being injured or paralyzed in an accident, was it meant to be or simply fate or bad timing? Certainly a question I have asked many times over the years.

The book includes captivating stories of people who have suffered horrible experiences in this lifetime. Working with a medium as a facilitator and guide, Schwartz takes them to the time on the soul plane when they are planning their next incarnation on earth. Through the medium he is able to see each soul sitting with their guides and soul family drawing out an intricate blueprint of all it will experience during its next lifetime. From birth to death, the people who will be a part of that existence, including parents, teachers, spouses and more; the events and encounters, are all elaborately orchestrated to give the soul the experience it desires. For many, that experience might deal with grief and loss, for some it is learning to adapt and thrive after a debilitating accident. And yet for others, perhaps it is the opportunity to experience the lack of mobility and voice that they had denied others in a previous lifetime. Each story describes not only the person's experience now in this physical plane, but also the soul's purpose.

Kristi told me in that very first reading that we agreed to do this and that it had more to do with my soul's evolution than hers. I can just imagine myself, the eager student still on the other side, a world devoid of suffering and loss saying, "Yes. I can handle this. Of course, piece of cake. Bring it on!"

The bad new is, once we arrive here on this earthly plane, we conveniently forget the plan, the reason behind the events we have chosen to experience. I guess it makes sense. How else would we really feel them, if we already knew the script? They need to be felt deeply, emotionally, and fully in order for our soul to grow.

In *As You Like It,* Shakespeare wrote, "All the world's a stage." Interesting theory—every person, every thing, every experience in our lives is part of our creation. We are the stars of our own movie, and everyone else a supporting actor to our leading lady or man. What do we want to learn, know, experience, and understand now? And so we design this intricate reality with a variety of characters and sub plots, solely for our own growth and evolution. It's a fascinating concept when you think about it. I love this quote by Shirley MacLaine: "I think of life itself now as a wonderful play that I've written for myself . . . and so my purpose is to have the utmost fun playing my part."

Kathy Overholt, a co-worker who left this world several years ago after a long bout with cancer, shared her thoughts with me shortly before she died.

"As I look back on my life, I can clearly see the hand of God, orchestrating, supporting, and guiding me," she told me.

She wrote the following poem. It was her final gift to those who had shared her life.

Single white calla lily with greens.
I believe I have emerged from this life of challenge and joys into
the presence of God with a clearer, purer vision of the soul
I was created to be.
Thank you for being part of my transformation.
Your words, your prayers, actions, and expressions of love
and concern strengthened my days.
I have always believed we are the product of ones around us.
You shaped, molded and contributed to who I am
and I am blessed by your presence.
I have taken the span of time allotted to me and been enriched
by my family, friends, and life experiences.
My joy in everyday things, like the beauty of a spring rain,
is as deep and abiding as my appreciation for
the wealth of companions in my life
and delight with adventures in places strange and wonderful.
My life has been full and rich with love.
I leave you not with regret at the abbreviation
of my span of time,
but with the joy in one whose life has been rich and fulfilling.
Find your joy and let it illuminate the days of your life.

— Kathy Overholt – February 9, 2002

Where are you Kristi?

We live in Colorado for God's sake.

There are plenty of mountains here.

I have been searching everywhere for you.

Four years is a long time.

Was your message simply a tease?

Are you really going to meet me at the base of some mountain?

I don't know what to believe any more.

Please Kristi, I will go anywhere just to be with you again.

CHAPTER 14

Voices in My Head

"Some people hear their own inner voices
with great clearness.
And they live by what they hear.
Such people become crazy... or they become legend."
- Jim Harrison

Chirp. The odd sound nudges me awake. *Chirp.* It happens again. *What is that?* The rattle of my lampshade next to the bed is the final prod.

"Ok, I'm awake. Who's there?"

"You need to get in your car and drive to Shambhala and bring your brochures," the voice says to me clearly, though not out loud but in my head.

"I can't go to Shambhala now, its 3:00 am."

The command is repeated. "You need to get in your car and drive to Shambhala and bring your brochures."

The voice is referring to Shambhala Mountain Center, a Buddhist retreat located in the mountains north of Fort Collins.

Established in 1971 by Tibetan meditation master and teacher Chögyam Trungpa Rinpoche, it is home to the Great Stupa of Dharmakaya, one of the most significant examples of sacred architecture in the world. The Great Stupa is a breathtaking structure that rises out of this remote wooded area; the ground upon which it stands is sacred.

"Ok, I'll go. But I can't go now. It's 3:00 am! And I can't go tomorrow, I have too many appointments. I can go Friday. Will that work?"

I am talking back to this voice in my head like it is an everyday occurrence. Truth is I am more than a little shaky; I have never really gotten contacted like this before. Somehow I come to the understanding that Friday will work. *Ok, I'm going to Shambhala on Friday, now what? And why am I to bring my brochures for the upcoming speaker series BellaSpark is producing?* I think maybe I will call my friend Lee; she lives in the area and I am pretty sure she has Fridays off.

"Anne," the voice says. "Anne will go with you and she will drive."

This is getting weirder by the moment. I decide to call my friend Anne instead of Lee, waiting at least until after 9:00 a.m. No sense in both of us being woken up in the middle of the night.

"Do you want to go to Shambhala on Friday?" I pose the question to Anne the following morning, not yet willing to give her an explanation of why I am planning this little expedition.

"I'd love to go. I haven't been there in ages and I've been thinking I need to spend some time there. My husband is out of town; I have his SUV, I'll drive," she replies.

Of course she will.

Well there it is. I am going to Shambhala because a voice in my head said I needed to go. It is only my second real message from an entity, spirit, whatever you want to call it—the first being the voice that told me to quit my job. At least this voice didn't instruct me to sell my house, cash in my 401k and give it all to some guru, or tell me to go to India and live in an ashram. I can handle a one-hour drive to the mountains. Shambhala is, after all, a magical place. Who knows what might happen there.

For a brief minute I allow myself to hope that maybe this is the mountain Kristi was talking about. Maybe that's why it is so important for me to go there. I will finally meet Kristi. Maybe. I close my eyes and pray.

It's interesting. When I tell Bob about my experience the next morning, he too doesn't question the validity.

"Well, I guess you're going to Shambhala on Friday," he says.

What is going on here? My husband never talks like that. He still thinks this stuff is crazy.

Anne and I head out early Friday morning. It is winter and the threat of snow becomes more and more ominous as we drive out of town and into the foothills. The drive up Poudre Canyon is beautiful. Once lush and green, the canyon wears its winter coat of brown now, patches of bright white snow contrasting starkly with the dormant winter vegetation. The canyon is ancient, formed by glacier and kept deep by the rapid waters of the Cache la Poudre River with sides of sheer granite soaring 3,000 feet above, dwarfing all below. The river is quiet today, sleepily flowing along under a blanket of ice.

We turn off the highway at the sign pointing to Shambhala and follow the narrow twisting dirt road, conscious that even with a 4-wheel drive vehicle we might want to head home before the snow hits. The entrance to Shambhala is non-descript, no big sign announcing this wonder of the world, no grand gate, just another pothole-filled dirt road.

Parking in the main lot, we begin the trek up to the Stupa, a winding path lined with faded colored flags. The wind is bitter cold and the flags, like attendants guiding the way, whip furiously. We pass the main building and though the lights are on there isn't a soul in sight—apparently we are the only ones on a pilgrimage today. Periodically we get a glimpse of the top of the Stupa through the trees and then it disappears again. Like a sporadic beacon from a lighthouse, it teases us and beckons us on. In summer, the trail is lined with yurts and tents, lodging for the many seekers who attend the various retreats and conferences hosted by the center. Today it looks barren and lonely. About three quarters of the way we come across a small building, a store of sorts. The lights are on and we welcome the opportunity to get out of the stinging wind.

"Anyone here?" we ask.

Once again, we are met with silence. The place is empty. We peruse the shelves—a few books on Buddhism and information about the Stupa but not much else. *Must be the slow season.* The entire place is eerily quiet and we are starting to feel as if we have been dropped into a sci-fi movie or something.

Sufficiently warm, we head out again. The Stupa rises out of the forest like a giant turban colorfully adorned in gold, red, and blue.

We climb the steps and respectfully take off our shoes before opening the massive doors guarding the entrance. We are greeted by a giant gold Buddha. Over 18-feet tall, he sits with a welcoming smile; one is instantly at peace here. Soft candles flicker around the space, small cushions and kneelers are carefully positioned for contemplation. We are the only ones in the Buddha's presence today. Wordlessly, we each find a place to sit and begin our own meditations. I am not sure what to expect. *Is the voice going to talk to me again? Am I going to experience some amazing awakening? Is Kristi going to come to me?*

"Well that was interesting," Anne remarks as we prepare to leave the temple. We emerge from the warmth of the gold Buddha to a world of snow. "Did you get any more information on why we are here?"

"No. No voices, no messages about why we are here. Whoopi Goldberg showed up in my meditation though," I reply.

I don't share with her my disappointment about not seeing Kristi. I guess this is not the mountain we are supposed to meet at after all. *What the hell is Whoopi Goldberg doing in my meditation? And what am I supposed to do with my brochures?*

The snow is coming down harder now. We are both thinking about the drive home and know it would be wise to hit the road and head back while we can. We decide to drop off the handful of my brochures at the little bookstore and the visitor's center at the main entrance. Again, we encounter no one. I think of a reference to parallel universes and multiple realities in one of the books I have been reading. If this is one of those places, perhaps it is time we left. I guess we did what we came for, we drop off the brochures and head to our car.

I am reminded of the book *The Five People You Meet in Heaven* by Mitch Albom. It follows the life and death of a maintenance man named Eddie. In a heroic attempt to save a little girl from falling off an amusement park ride, Eddie is killed and sent to heaven where he encounters five people who significantly impacted him and whom he, in turn, affected while he was alive. The underlying message of the story rings true with me: there are no random acts in life. We touch thousands of people, often unaware we are having an impact. I hope someone will be touched in some way by my brochures at Shambhala.

Who knows who will be impacted by our actions today? There is always a reason why we do the things we do. Life is all about having faith in that inner voice that guides us. We instinctively know when something feels right or not, we just need to listen and follow our intuition. Sometimes that voice may show up in unexpected ways. We have to trust it even when we don't know where it's leading us. There is a bigger picture, one much grander than the tiny screen we are able to see with our human eyes. I am learning to have faith in those messages, even when I don't understand. God has a much bigger plan for me.

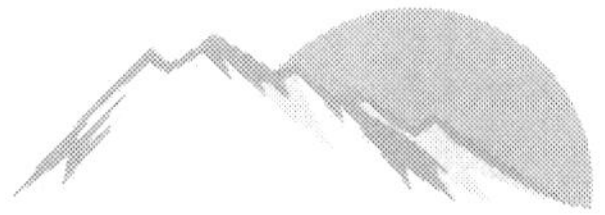

CHAPTER 15

No Stranger to Death

"Old as she was, she still missed her daddy sometimes".
- Gloria Naylor

I am no stranger to death. My father died when I was fifteen. Kristi's death had forced me to revisit that loss. *What is the lesson here? What am I to learn from this grief? Did I not figure it out the first time, is that why I need to experience this again? What do you want from me God?*

It was one of those typical Wisconsin winters of the time, lots of snow that year. I had just turned 15. I don't remember my birthday. In fact, I don't remember much about that year, except one thing. My birthday is January 8 and here it was just a couple weeks later, January 25. As a freshman in high school, I had a good year. That fall I had made the B squad cheerleading team, had lots of great friends, and was elected president of the freshman class. My dad helped me write my campaign speech. Life was good.

It had snowed heavily the night before. Two-foot drifts filled the driveway but it was Wisconsin and school rarely closed for snow days. My sisters and brother and I usually had shovel duty, clearing out as much as we could before heading off to school. I was sick with a bad cold and excused from school, so I stayed in bed while they shoveled what they could. Dad would finish the rest.

"Donna, come up here … "

It took me a while to recognize the voice. Sound asleep and buried under a mound of blankets in my basement bedroom, my mother was calling me. Her voice was quiet, but something in her tone told me to come now. I came upstairs to find my father lying on the floor, unconscious with a strange sound coming from his mouth.

Death rattle . . .

"Call the ambulance. He was shoveling snow. He just came in, and then collapsed."

Before the advent of CPR, neither of us knew what to do. We just watched him lay there with this rattled breathing sound. *What is taking them so long?*

Eventually the rattled breathing stopped. It felt like hours, but it was probably only a few minutes.

Helpless, we waited.

Finally, we heard the siren of the ambulance and then the flashing lights were at the end of our long driveway. It was another couple minutes before the driver could maneuver it up the still snow-covered drive. A man came to the door, apologizing for the delay. And then he saw my dad. He knew that he was too late, but he made an attempt anyway. He gave a sharp blow to the chest, then another; nothing. He went back outside and returned with a stretcher. Somehow, I don't remember now, we must have gotten my father onto the stretcher and he took him out to the waiting ambulance.

"Call Pastor John," my mom said as she bundled up and headed out the door. She climbed into the back of the ambulance next to my dad. And they were gone.

I watched from the window. There were no sirens this time.

Alone, I looked up the phone number for our pastor.

"Something happened to my father. The ambulance took him to the hospital," I told him, giving the impression that my dad had fallen ill, but I knew that wasn't the case. I knew in my heart my words were a lie, but I couldn't utter the "D" word, not yet. *My father is not dead!*

There was no one else to call. No grandparents, no aunts and uncles close by. It had always been just us, two parents, five kids, and occasionally a dog.

I waited. I didn't cry. Not yet.

It had been over an hour. *What should I do? Get dressed. You will need to be dressed when they return.* I sat, alone.

My mom returned, driven by our pastor. She was silent. Pastor John told me what I already knew.

"I went to the hospital emergency room looking for your father. I had to wander all over the hospital until I found him in the morgue," he admonished. I just looked at him.

He called the schools to tell them to bring my sisters and brother home. When they arrived, they knew something was up . . . and it was not good. I looked at them silently as they filed in. The pastor gathered us all in the living room and delivered the bad news. He used the "D" word.

Many of the memories escape me now, buried in some deep recess of my heart. Perhaps they are safe there. One memory stands out clearly though: my mom standing at the kitchen counter making phone calls to the relatives. "Culver's gone," she said. And then explained, over and over, to the brothers, sister, aunts and uncles. She didn't use the "D" word.

It took a while for the relatives to arrive. Within a day or two, they descended on us, filling the house with their tears, their condolences, their memories, their stories, their ideas on how we should proceed. I just wished they would leave. It had always been just us, my parents and five kids. Periodically, my mom's parents would show up for a visit, or we would connect with one of my father's siblings and our cousins. All lived far from us. But mostly it was just us. Holidays, birthdays, special occasions, we were our own team, our own support system. Our family was us, and my dad was not only our leader, but our foundation.

After my father's death, my mom had to navigate on her own. I never realized how young she was until just recently, looking at my own grown children, at my son and his wife who are 38. To me they are young and vibrant. My mother was 38 when my dad died.

My father was the center of our universe; five demanding children, all wanting to be his favorite. My brother Mike had it easy; the lone boy in the family, his status of favored son was secure. My youngest sister, Susie, the baby of the family, also held a special spot. That left the three oldest girls to wrangle for position. There is my sister Mary, the first born, steady, dependable, didn't rock the boat; Patty, sister number three, the middle child in the family who grabbed her attention by getting into the most trouble; and me, the overachiever.

I still vaguely recall the dream I had shortly after my father died. A wonderful combination of my father and Jesus, I did not want to leave that place of absolute love and fought to remain in it even as my mom called me to get up for school. I did not want to wake up, ever. When finally awake, I struggled to remember the details. All I remember is my dad and Jesus, together.

People ask me if I honestly think psychics are real. I admit I am so desperate to connect with my daughter that I will believe anything that gives me a feeling that she is still with me. And yes, some of the messages I get are fairly generic: she loves me, she is happy, she is with me, don't be sad. I guess, anyone could state that and I would tend to believe they are talking to Kristi. But sometimes, things are said and shared that leave no doubt in my mind that this is real; my loved ones do exist in a different dimension and they are still watching over me.

I am attending another group class for people who want to enhance their psychic and intuitive abilities. Michael is one of the instructor's regular students. I had met him briefly on one other occasion. As the class starts, he turns to me and says, "There's a man standing over my shoulder, I think this is your father. He's wearing a business suit and hat."

"Sounds like my dad," I say.

"He has a crooked smile," Michael goes on to tell me.

My jaw drops.

"He had ear surgery when he was a child and it damaged a nerve. His mouth droops a little on one side," he continues.

Wow! No one would know that. How could he know this about my father?

Michael then goes on to describe the day my father died, the deep snow, shoveling the driveway, coming in for a break, sitting at the kitchen table, clutching his chest, falling to the floor. Michael doesn't know me and he certainly wouldn't know anything about my father's death almost forty years before.

"Your father wants you to know there was nothing you could do. It was a massive heart attack; you could not have saved him. And, there was a reason you were there."

When you get a message like that, from someone who has no clue about who you are, where you come from, your history, you know in your heart this is not bullshit.

I realize I have been carrying guilt about my father's death for almost forty years. I blame myself; how does one even begin to release that? I ask myself over and over, why was I there? It makes sense that my father did not want to die alone so he chose a day when my mother would be home from work. And he probably did not want my mother to be alone either, but why me? Why was I the one home sick that day and not my brother or one of my sisters?

"Because you are the strong one, Donna. You are the chosen one, the one who agreed to take on this role. The experiences, the lessons, the wisdom gained, are all part of your soul's path," an inner voice tells me.

I realize I am still angry. Angry with him for leaving me, angry that he wasn't there to steer me through my teenage and young adult years, during those times I was making life decisions. You *should have been there to guide me, to help me. My choices might have been different.* I don't want to be the strong one!

"I didn't do everything right, Donna," my father speaks to me again through Michael.

"Yes you did," I respond. "You loved me. You encouraged me. You believed in me, like no one else. And then you left me."

It dawns on me that I still see my father through the eyes of a child and I understand now that I never really knew him as an adult. I put him on a pedestal and trusted everything I learned from him to be gospel. I did not know his fears, his faults, his weaknesses. I knew him only as a parent—sometimes fun and relaxed, often strict. Too strict in my teenage mind. Yet, he was the person I looked up to and relied on. After he died, as a teenager, cocky and arrogant and struggling to become independent, I told myself that everything was okay; I knew what I was doing and it didn't matter. It's only now that I begin to realize how events can color one's life.

It's been five years since Kristi left this world, though sometimes it feels like yesterday. I still long to pick up the phone and hear her voice saying, "Hey, what are you doing?" And I am still searching for the mountain, in fact, it is getting more intense, a sense of urgency engulfs me. I scrutinize everywhere I go. Is there a mountain there? Is this the place? Is Kristi still waiting for me?

I am flying into Seattle. For once there is a break in the thick heavy clouds and I am able to observe majestic Mount Rainier. We are flying so close one can see the snow-covered peak, craggy rocks and the thick evergreen of the forest. It is breathtakingly beautiful, yet so out of reach.

I know you are with me Kristi. I feel your energy and hear your voice in my head. But it's not the same. I can't see you and touch you.

Is this the mountain Kristi? I will go there if you promise to meet me.

CHAPTER 16

Dream Big

"Life is short, live bold!
Be heard, be you, dream big, take risks, don't wait."
~ Misty Gibbs

It is time for me to dream again. Somewhere along the way I learned to believe that life is limited, that we only are allowed so many wishes. Perhaps it was the Genie in the Bottle story where you only get three wishes. Maybe it was the parents who always said, "Money doesn't grow on trees," or the teacher who said, "You're not cut out for that." As a child, I remember dreaming and fantasizing what my life would be like; it seems like a million years ago. To be honest, I can't remember the last time I dreamed of all the things I wanted, things I wanted to do and see, things I wanted to have in my life. When did I learn to limit myself?

Have you ever noticed how often we start off with a big dream, a vision that is so clear in our mind, we know it is ours to have? Initially we work toward that dream, do whatever it takes to accomplish it, we are moving forward full speed ahead. And then we start listening to the voices in our head, the ones that say, "You're not smart enough, you can't afford that, you'll never accomplish that." And so we let our dream fall to the wayside, as we have so many times in the past.

We live in a limitless universe, and all that we want is available to us, as long as we believe that it can be ours. Why is it so hard for us to believe that health, abundance, and love belong to us all?

One of my favorite movies that I used to watch with our children and now watch with our grandchildren is *The Never Ending Story*. The film is about a little boy, Bastian, with a vivid imagination who loves to read. He is often admonished to get his head out of the clouds. One day he is given a special book, a magnificent story about the quirky and beautiful Kingdom of Fantasia that is slowly being destroyed by The Nothing. As Bastian reads he gradually becomes part of the story.

Bastian is carried along in the story as The Nothing gobbles up the kingdom. He joins the young hero Atreyu as he tries to save the kingdom but alas, Atreyu succumbs to The Nothing as well. In one of the final scenes, there is nothing left of the kingdom but the young princess of Fantasia and a single grain of sand. The princess tells Bastian that he holds the key to bringing the kingdom back. All he has to do is make a wish.

"How many wishes do I get?" whispers Bastian.

"As many as you want," replies the Princess.

I think of that line often as I struggle to become the creator of my own life. Often I feel a need to limit what I wish for, curb my focus to only one thing at a time, convinced that the Universe will grant me only one wish. I can still hear Bastian's voice asking the question, "How many wishes do I get?" and especially the Princess' reply, "As many as you want."

Yes, it is time for me to dream again. I have a vision for

BellaSpark: to make this wonderful information available to the world, to reach as many people as I can. I am determined to dream big and large, to make as many wishes as I like. My list will be long and bold and magnificent. I will write my wishes and affirmations down and repeat them everyday. I am, after all, like Bastion, the creator of my kingdom.

CHAPTER 17

It's All About the Energy

"Love is like energy.
It can never be created nor destroyed
. . . it is just always there."
- Ian Philpot

More and more I tend to receive communication from my guides when in or near water. Soaking in the bathtub late at night is one of my favorite things to do. With a profusion of candles flickering softly, quiet music playing in the background, it is the perfect way to unwind and reconnect to my higher self and Spirit, and to write. With a tablet and pen handy, I jot down the messages that come to me. Often I will compose an article for BellaSpark magazine or my blog. It's an interesting endeavor to say the least, as water drips on the paper leaving large splotches of smeared ink on the page. As a result, my notes can be difficult to decipher the next day and I struggle to remember the message that came to me so clearly the night before. *What was it you were telling me?* I ask my guides, hoping they will be patient with me and fill in the details. My friend Linda likes to hold her morning meditation while soaking in her hot tub. She, too, finds that connection is easier when immersed in water.

Again a message came to me while in the shower. That morning I had asked to know the purpose of the events I was producing. Immediately the image of an atomic bomb exploding popped into my head. "It's all about the energy," the message came in, loud and clear. I saw a giant mushroom cloud and the resulting shock wave spreading across the atmosphere. The fallout drifted across the countryside, changing the landscape from dark to vibrant as it traveled. The image was not one of destruction, my guides were quick to assure me, rather, it was a metaphor for how the energy created at these events expands and flows across the planet.

The idea that everything is energy, including us, is an interesting concept. Though our physical bodies and the chair we are sitting on may look and feel solid, they are in fact nothing more than a collection of atoms—microscopic particles of protons, electrons, and neutrons—vibrating rapidly to form a tangible shape. Much like a water molecule which when cooled and slowed enough becomes ice, we, too, as spiritual beings have lowered our vibration in order to appear in physical form in this dimension of time and space.

The really fascinating part is that our words and our thoughts are also energy. The product generated from our thoughts and emotions is emitted as energy. It carries a frequency much like an FM radio signal or a satellite signal, and though we cannot see the signal, it is being transmitted to the world in the same manner. That signal, that emotional energy, is then reflected back at us to create the world we see and experience.

The movie *The Celestine Prophecy* does a really good job of visually showing how energy works as our thoughts flow out and interact with another's. In the film, people's thoughts are depicted in color and we are able to see how they intermingle with another's field and the effect they have on that person, whether that person is conscious of it or not. Most of us can recall walking into a room and feeling uncomfortable or sensing a heaviness that makes us want to leave. We may have also experienced a feeling of lightness emanating from a space where the occasion is joyous.

We like to think that our thoughts are hidden; no one knows what they are. The truth is that our thoughts can affect others, on an unconscious level, just as we are affected by the thoughts and energy of others. Over the years we have seen examples of crowd mentality, how the energy of even one person can transform a crowd of people into an angry mob. The media is especially good at working us into a negative state. When fed a constant diet of depressing and pessimistic news, it's no wonder we are filled with fear, frustration, anger, and polarization. The world we live in is a reflection of our unconscious mind, the collective thoughts and emotions of seven billion people creating the world we experience.

The energy we send out can also work in a more positive way. Like the ever-expanding ripples across water when an object is dropped into it, we can create a ripple effect with our energy. I first began to understand this concept while hosting an event with Dr. Wayne Dyer. While standing on the stage introducing him to the audience, I could see in my mind's eye the affirmative energy created by the over 2,300 like-minded spiritual seekers in attendance. It undulated out from the arena as it spread across Colorado and over the Eastern plains like a gentle breeze rippling the wheat fields as it steadfastly worked its way across the landscape. I knew we were sending love and light around the planet and that it couldn't help but leave something positive in its wake.

Again the energy was obvious the night Michael Bernard Beckwith came to Fort Collins for a BellaSpark event. With the enthusiasm of a charismatic revivalist minister and rapid-fire speech, Michael can be a little intimidating at first. "I talk fast because, though your conscious mind might not comprehend what I am saying, the subconscious gets it completely," Michael told the audience. I could feel their trepidation as Michael began, but soon the energy began to grow and by the end of the night it had exploded. The entire hall was on its feet singing *Jeremiah Was a Bullfrog* with Ricki Byers Beckwith and proclaiming, "Yes I can!" along with Michael. As the crowd exited the building that evening, it seemed as if they were floating above the ground. Something powerful had happened and the groundswell of love and light produced by over a thousand people was rippling out from the center of Fort Collins and being broadcast through the airwaves, shifting the consciousness of the planet.

We interact with many people. If we change our energy—and it in turn changes the energy of two other people, and so on, and so on—the ripple effect can be powerful beyond our knowing. I truly believe that we are all connected and that each and every one of us has the power to create change.

Have you heard of the Butterfly Effect? It is based on the theory that a small change in one place can result in large differences in another. An example would be when a butterfly flaps its wings in Colorado, a hurricane happens in Miami. The name of the effect, coined by Edward Lorenz, is derived from the theoretical example of a hurricane's formation being contingent on whether or not a distant butterfly had flapped its wings several weeks earlier.

The following is a story about Susan and Tom and how the butterfly effect came into play in a positive way.

Susan got off to a late start one morning and still had to pick up donuts on the way to work. Her boss had called a big staff meeting with the president of the company in attendance and he wanted to make a good impression. Susan was stressed as she rushed around the grocery store picking out the donuts; she was anxious to get out of there quickly. But when she got to the check out line, of course only one lane was open and in front of her was Tom with a full cart of groceries. Susan thought, "Dang, I'm going to be late!" But Tom, upon seeing that Susan looked a little harried, graciously agreed to let her go first.

With that, Susan was able to get to the office in plenty of time. She got the coffee going, arranged the donuts nicely on a tray, and made sure her boss, Bill, got the crème-filled one he really liked; the meeting went off without a hitch. So now Susan's boss was happy, he made a good impression on the company president, and it was a good day all around.

That afternoon Bill got a call from Joe, a customer. They had been involved in a dispute over some equipment for quite some time. Well, Bill was in such a good mood he was willing to work with Joe and they came to an amicable agreement. Now Joe was happy.

A couple hours later Joe, who happened to work in the poultry business, got a call from the food bank. They were really short on turkeys for their Thanksgiving baskets that year. Could Joe help them out? He was feeling generous because he was able to work things out with his supplier and said, "Sure. How many do you need?"

Now the food bank had plenty of turkeys to fill their Thanksgiving baskets. They put in a call to Mary, one of their clients. Mary had been worrying about Thanksgiving. She had been laid off from her job six months prior and was unable to find work; with a family of three children it had been difficult for Mary to put food on the table. Mary knew there wasn't anything in her pantry for Thanksgiving dinner. Now Mary had a turkey and a big basket with all the fixings.

So there it was. Tom, our little butterfly, with his single act of kindness to Susan that morning, just put Thanksgiving dinner on the table for Mary!

A simple story, but it demonstrates how we are all butterflies. Every day we touch people in multiple ways. Most of the time, we have no idea what kind of impact we have. But the power of ONE is an incredible force and when we recognize our connection to each other, it becomes second nature to flap our wings in a manner that brings about the highest good for all, including ourselves. For that which we do unto others, we do unto ourselves.

It makes one think. What is the energy we are emitting? What kind of world are we creating with our thoughts, words, and deeds? I love this definition of the word Universe: uni, meaning One; verse, meaning Song. One Song! Imagine for a moment that we are just one note in a giant symphony called life . . . one tiny note in this composition. No matter how we separate into individual little notes, we are still involved in the One Song. Through our collective energy we are composing a symphony; let's make it a beautiful one.

CHAPTER 18

Synchronicity

"We do not create our destiny;
we participate in its unfolding.
Synchronicity works as a catalyst
toward the working out of that destiny."
- David Richo

Have you ever had uncanny incidents happen to you? You think of someone for the first time in years and run into that person a few hours later. A word or phrase jumps out at you three times in the same day and leads you in a direction you hadn't planned. A book falls off the shelf at the bookstore and it's exactly what you need. My husband calls them coincidences, though even he has to admit at times some circumstances are just too strange to be mere happenstance.

Those mysterious events are called synchronicity and are more powerful and meaningful to our lives than we realize. The dictionary defines synchronicity as an uncanny coincidence, the unlikely conjunction of events, or a startling serendipity. Who hasn't had synchronicity in his or her life? We wonder how it happens. Where does it come from? Perhaps it is from the unseen realms. Is it so difficult to believe that our guardian angels, guides and loved ones with their all-seeing perspective from the other side are actively involved in guiding us on our right path? When we pay attention and are open to Spirit's guidance, it is amazing how things can line up for us.

I find that synchronicity shows itself more and more in my life as I open to it. It is quite magical and I am often delighted when I encounter it, and sometimes quite surprised at the direction in which it leads me. I like to think Kristi is my partner in this BellaSpark venture, that she actually has a vested interest in its success since it was her leaving that was the catalyst for its birth. I talk to her often, asking for guidance, trusting that she is helping me from the other side, orchestrating things to unfold perfectly. It reminds me that Kristi and Spirit are guiding me always; I just need to listen and allow.

BellaSpark was expanding. For quite some time now I had been feeling a nudge to take the Extraordinary People Series to Seattle. My sister Patty lived there; I knew I could stay with her. I figured it would be an easy transition to a larger market, there should be lots of people in Seattle who were also hungry for this information.

My first series was to begin in January 2008. Lining up speakers was always an interesting process as I juggled speaker schedules and limited dates at the performance hall. I started with some of my favorites: John Holland, Alan Cohen, Iyanla Vanzant, and Gregg Braden, but still needed a fifth speaker; with nothing coming together I was running out of options, not sure who to contact next.

Please help me, I plead to Kristi, my Angels, my guides. *Bring me the final speaker for the Seattle series, I am running out of time.*

Working both on the new Seattle series as well as events for Fort Collins kept me busy. Contacting this speaker and that agent or assistant, and trying to develop a relationship with people who don't know me could be challenging to say the least. Unfortunately, when you are new to producing events, it is sometimes difficult to get your foot in the door. Often the response sounded like, "Who the hell are you?" I was beginning to understand. After all, these folks were in big demand. It was important for them that the producers they were working with knew their stuff.

I was still hoping to bring Deepak Chopra to Fort Collins. He was not only one of the leaders in the new thought and holistic health arena, but man, what a coup that would be! I had called and written Deepak's office several times with no response. No harm in trying one more time. My goal was to book Deepak for an event in Fort Collins in the fall of 2009. This time when I called, I got an answer. Deepak's assistant was actually familiar with BellaSpark—wow, that's a step in the right direction. She was impressed with the speakers we had brought in so far and the size of the crowds we had drawn. This was starting to look good. I told her about my expansion to Seattle, hoping to convince her that we were a large organization and knew what we are doing.

"But," she said, "we are not scheduling that far out. I will have to get back to you next year."

Sure sounded like a put-off to me. So when the phone rang two days later, I was surprised to hear her voice.

"I bet you didn't expect to hear from me so soon," she remarked.

She went on to tell me Deepak was doing a book tour after the first of the year and wondered if I would be interested in having him as part of my speaker series in Seattle.

"I might be interested," I responded, trying to sound cool. *Interested, are you kidding me? Kick off my series in Seattle with Deepak Chopra in the line up? Of course I'm interested!*

Turns out Deepak would be in Seattle on Tuesday, March 4, 2008, the exact date I had reserved at the performance hall. Of course he would. I couldn't believe it. BellaSpark Productions and Deepak Chopra—the Universe was definitely working for me!

Thank you Kristi, Angels, guides. You are the best!

It was the day before New Years Eve, 2007. I was enjoying lunch at my favorite Chinese restaurant with two young women I had recently met. Kat and Maru are both psychics. This was our first meeting, and we spent a lot of time learning about each other, our backgrounds, how we started on this path, and where we saw ourselves going. I told them that BellaSpark was kicking off a new series in Seattle beginning in January 2008 and that I was considering adding another city in 2009, probably somewhere in the Midwest. The conversation continued like that for a while as we visited and enjoyed our lunch.

Out of the blue and in the middle of taking another bite of her Kung Pao chicken, Maru declared, "You know you're going to Vancouver next. You might think you're going to the Midwest, but you're going to Vancouver."

Well, Vancouver was not even on my radar. In fact, I have never been there and wasn't even sure where it was. I laugh and file her comment away in the crazy psychic file.

The following day as luck would have it, I woke up with the

stomach flu; so much for my plans to go out for New Year's Eve dinner with my husband and drink champagne. I spent most of the day either in the bathroom or in bed. Late afternoon my cell phone rang. The caller was asking about the Seattle series: how to purchase tickets, questions about the various guest speakers, etc. She was quite the Chatty Cathy and very excited about our lineup. Since I had nothing better to do, we talked for several minutes.

"I can't wait to see these people. I'm coming down for every one!" she proclaimed.

"Where do you live?" I asked.

"Vancouver."

As I hung up the phone I looked to the heavens. "Ok. I get the message. I guess I'm going to Vancouver next!"

The caller, Karen Elkins did drive down from Vancouver for every show that season. She became not only a good friend, but my partner, helping create BellaSpark events in Vancouver.

I love it when the Universe brings me direct signs like this one. I must be a little dense, or walk around with blinders on, because if my guides are sending me cues and signs all the time, I don't always catch them. This is my kind of message. *Thank you, Angels.*

It is always interesting to see how things unfold, what mysteries Spirit has to share with me. It was early October and I was getting ready for don Miguel Ruiz's arrival in Fort Collins. His book *The Four Agreements*, so simple yet so profound, had touched my soul. There was something special about this man, gentle and loving, unassuming and gracious. He gave the most amazing hugs; you yearned to stay in his embrace forever. I was so excited I could hardly stand it.

I was surprised to find out, when all the arrangements were complete, that Miguel was coming in a day early. With an extra day to fill, I was determined to show him a good time. A beautiful fall day, the morning was crisp and cool, the bright sun holding promise of a beautiful afternoon. We decided to take a drive up Poudre Canyon and enjoy the sites; the aspen trees were decked out in brilliant gold, a sharp contrast to the deep forest green of the pines. We saw the sign for Shambhala Mountain Center, the same spot I had my weird experience a while back, and since Miguel had never been to Shambhala, we decided to check it out. This time the place was busy—numerous spiritual seekers meditating quietly in the Stupa, walking the grounds, enjoying the serenity of this sacred place. We entered the Stupa and found a comfortable place for our own contemplation. Immediately the voice in my head was loud and clear: "Thank you for bringing him here. It is time for him to merge his energies with ours."

In my mind's eye I saw pockets of light scattered around the globe—divine energy locations—each distinct, some brighter than others. Like twinkling stars, they brought light to an otherwise dark world. I got an image of them gradually connecting, ringing the earth in all directions until the entire planet was once again illuminated with radiant healing energy. Don Miguel carried ancient Toltec lineage and there was certainly a powerful energy force at Shambhala. It made perfect sense that these two forces were to connect.

I found out afterwards that when trying to make airline reservations, Miguel was unable to come in on the scheduled date as planned. No matter what airline they tried, between various times and different connections, nothing seemed to work. Again Spirit was leading us, a Divine purpose perfectly orchestrated.

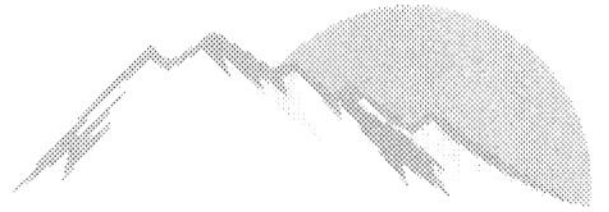

Chapter 19

Finding the Guru in Us

"The teacher who is indeed wise does not bid you to enter the house of his wisdom but rather leads you to the threshold of your mind."
~ Kahlil Gibran

The Seattle Series is a month away and I am getting nervous. I have reserved a really big hall. *What if I don't get enough people?* I am on the hook for big bucks here. My empty credit card is not so empty anymore. *What was I thinking?* I start to panic. Meditating, hoping I will get some guidance or insight, I ask for help.

"Kristi, Angels, please let me know if I am on the right track. Just give me a sign."

This time I am sure it is Kristi's voice I hear in my head and she is none too gentle with me. *"We gave you Deepak Chopra, for God's sake. What more do you want? Quit your whining!"*

Guess I got my answer.

Producing events can be risky business. At times I am terrified. I regularly lay my future on the line, running up credit cards, making deposits on venues and speakers, paying for advertising, and marketing, marketing, marketing. With each event I hope and pray that enough people will show up to cover my costs, even make some money. It is some of the hardest work I have ever done, and also the most rewarding.

Often I lay in bed at night, worrying about details and of course, money. I am trying hard to trust the Universe, to believe that this is the right path for me. I ask for guidance and confirmation often.

I tell myself that my work is to bring this information to the world, to plant the seeds for higher consciousness. At times I think I am just making it up. *Does anyone really care?*

I get my confirmation from many. A woman comes up to me at one of my events and thanks me for the speakers I have brought in; they have changed her life. Another shares that Caroline Myss was the catalyst for her to begin anew. Others let me know how much they like BellaSpark Magazine, or that the messages on my blog touch their heart. Many, many comments, they give me the courage to continue. I realize they, too, are searching for answers just as I am. I'm grateful for their feedback, if they only knew how much their appreciation means to me, supports me and buoys me up when I question myself.

I am traveling regularly now between Seattle, Vancouver and my home in Colorado. I spend many nights at my sister's in Seattle. Not on the same spiritual path as me, she rarely attends my events, though she does wait up for me, ready to celebrate the evening's success over a glass of wine. Patty and I talk late into the night, sharing childhood memories. We never talked much as a family, even after our father died, taking our cue from our mother who silently carried her burdens with stoic resolve. We learned early to bury our emotions, our grief. Our conversations are healing and I begin to grasp that my coming to Seattle with my speaker series is more about healing our family than the actual events themselves. I realize there is still much I have yet to understand about how this Universe works.

I am extremely blessed. I get to meet and work with extraordinary people. What's it like, working with such incredible visionaries? We tend to put these spiritual teachers on a pedestal, see them as our savior, the ones who can fix our problems. What I've learned is that they, too, are human. Just like us they also have their stuff—issues, challenges, and unreconciled beliefs. They are both magnificent conduits for Spirit when they are sharing their wisdom with an audience or through their books and workshops, as well as beautiful examples of human frailty. They offer us invaluable information and tools for understanding and navigating this often confusing spiritual path and I have indeed learned much. However, I have come to realize that the teachers we seek for guidance are there only to help us uncover that which we already know deep inside. Alan Cohen defines the word guru as "Gee You Are You," for everything we need to know is already hardwired in us; our job is to remember who we are and our capabilities as Divine Beautiful Sparks of God.

I am often amazed at the teachers who come into my life, both those who appear on stage and those who just show up in everyday life. It's as if some unseen conductor orchestrates exactly what I need to learn next and then leads me to the teacher. The gift these spiritual advisors bring me is always profound and I, in turn, want to share that gift with others.

I have been searching for six long years. A rational person would certainly be over this mountain thing by now. But here I am again, scrutinizing every location as I travel, questioning every message, asking, "Is this the mountain, Kristi?"

I am in Maui attending a Wayne Dyer conference. The energy on this small little island in the Pacific is amazing. I am told this was the site of Lemuria. The Legend of Lemuria is one of an ancient lost civilization that existed prior to and during the time of Atlantis. I can feel it.

Every morning I am woken up in a weird fashion. Sometimes I hear a voice, or funny chirp. One morning my little computer voice, the one that welcomes me to MSN when I log in, says "Good morning Donna." Funny thing though, my computer is turned off. My two roommates are sleeping soundly; it is, after all, only 5:00 a.m. They hear nothing. I know that the voice wants me to get up and meditate and walk on the beach.

It is beautiful here. There is a full moon this week and every morning I watch it set over the ocean. I am astonished by the number of people who are out at this time, meditating, doing yoga, some walking, some running in the sand, soaking up this incredible energy. I can see why my guides/angels want me out here. You can connect with them in a way that you aren't able to normally. My meditations are really good.

Today we are heading to a special place, a waterfall on the side of a mountain. The hillside is lush and green. This has to be Kristi's mountain. I search, I sit, I meditate, and I struggle to connect.

"Please Kristi, are you going to meet me here?"

Again, I am rebuffed. There is no sign of Kristi, no message, no dream, no big moment.

"Why Kristi? Why do you not meet me as promised? I don't understand."

Chapter 20
The Urge

"Have you ever been hurt and the place tries to heal a bit, and you just pull the scar off of it over and over again."
~ Rosa Parks

I still have the urge. I thought I had gotten over it, but there it was, welling up inside of me like molten lava breaking forth from deep underground. It surprises me. After all, it has been six years since Kristi died. I should be over this by now.

I am standing on the corner, at the side of the curb, when a semi truck drives by. And there it is; that familiar urge. To just step out into traffic, in front of the truck and put an end to it once and for all. How easy it would be. How pleasant, to finally close the door on the pain and grief and loss. I can go home. I can be with my beautiful daughter again.

Having talked to other parents who have lost children, I know that this is a common thought; the desire to end it all and be with your child again is sometimes overwhelming and one must stay in control in order to not act on it.

The waves of grief hit you hard. At first they are unrelenting, like a wild and stormy sea, knocking you down faster than you can stand up. But as time goes by the waves get further and further apart; the trough between them is wider and less deep. You still feel them, and they never quite go away. And every once in a while, out of the blue, they roar again, and you are once again drowning in their unrelenting sadness. It can be a year, five years, or ten, yet their sheer force still overwhelms you and threatens to drag you under. The difference is the storm doesn't last as long, the intensity lessens, and you realize you can endure once again. You will survive.

I try to live in the moment. I know that Kristi and I will be together again, that we are really not apart. I am not afraid of death, more so that it will take its own sweet time in choosing me. I have much to live for, yet to live perhaps thirty more years without one of my children seems unfathomable sometimes. I resist the urge once again, as I have for the past six years since Kristi left.

I think of my other children, my sons Jason and Adam and my daughter Jenny. Do they know that I love them just as much as Kristi? Do they know that if it had been any one of them, my pain would be as great? A mother's love is absolute; each of her children holds a special place in her heart. Yet the pain, the loss of loosing one of those children can be overwhelming at times, so much so that we might short-change those who are still with us. It is not what I mean to do, to make them feel less loved. To my children: know that I love you and value who you are, and appreciate your patience and support. I will never stop loving you.

Perhaps I do have more to do or learn on this soul's journey. But I will be ready, ready to go home, with open arms as soon as I am given the nod. And then I will follow the urge. I will step without hesitation into the path and allow myself to be run over, this time by the light. I will be Home once again.

CHAPTER 21
Gratitude

"Let us rise up and be thankful, for if we didn't learn a lot today, at least we learned a little, and if we didn't learn a little, at least we didn't get sick, and if we got sick, at least we didn't die; so, let us all be thankful."

\- Buddha

The snow is falling in Colorado. It is late night and quiet; so very quiet I can almost hear the voice of heaven. The responsibilities and to do list are far away, and if only for this moment I am immersed in the stillness. And I am thankful—thankful for the quiet, for the much-needed opportunity to slow down for a moment to clear the clutter and hush the never-ending cacophony in my brain.

It is the season for gratitude, a host of holidays all offering us the opportunity to express and share our appreciation for others. I find it incongruous that we need a season to be grateful, as if gratitude is something we wear once a year, like the holiday tie or sweater, then tuck back into the closet until the proper event requires its use again. Perhaps gratitude should be worn daily, loudly, and carefree, like a little boy's favorite baseball cap. Saying thank you proclaims to the Universe the world we wish to see. Poet Sarah Ban Breathnach writes, "You simply will not be the same person two months from now after consciously giving thanks each day for the abundance that exists in your life. And you will have set in motion an ancient spiritual law: The more you have and are grateful for, the more will be given you."

I have found that when I open myself to Spirit, amazing things happen. I not only find joy in the small things in life, but my connection to Spirit is so much easier.

One of the best ways to raise our connection to Spirit is through gratitude. It is a powerful way to bridge the vibrational gap between where we are and where we would like to be. There is a strong correlation between appreciation/gratitude and the Law of Attraction. Being grateful for what we have in our life, right here, right now, tells the Universe what we like and based on the Law of Attraction—that like attracts like—it is obliged to bring us more of what we are grateful for.

In addition, there is a growing body of scientific and academic research that backs up the important role gratitude can play in living a happier, healthier life. What would our life be like if we were to choose to be happy for no reason other than because the sun is shining, or because we can see with our eyes or smell the flowers, or have legs that allow us to take a walk?

Author Susan Jeffers suggests that to learn to be grateful, we should make a list of fifty things every evening that we are thankful for that day. They need not be big, in fact, it is more important they be small. Initially it may be difficult to come up with people, events, things, etc. that we might be grateful for. Often our mind is filled with all the little slights and annoyances that occurred throughout the day: the guy in the car who cut us off, the rude sales clerk at the grocery store, the grumbling boss who piles on extra work as we try to leave for the day, the telemarketer who calls just as we are sitting down to dinner. There are many little things that can rub us the wrong way.

I have to admit, completing the list was hard for me at first. Of course there were the usual choices: my family that includes my wonderful husband, my children and especially my three grandchildren; and my friends and the job that I loved. But over time as I worked at it, the list became longer and the listing got easier: a sunny Colorado day, a close-in parking space at the store, finding just the right pair of shoes, a funny email from a friend that made me laugh, the chocolate chip cookies a neighbor dropped off, a long hot shower in the morning, a bowl of popcorn and an ice-cold Coke, the five-dollar bill I found in my coat pocket that allowed me to go for a latte, the woman who gave me a pedicure—for that I was truly grateful, anyone who would touch these toes . . .

And then there is the gratitude that comes with acceptance. Yes, I still grieve for my daughter, but in the same light, I am grateful for the twenty-one years she shared with me and for all that she has given and taught me from the other side.

Another year has passed and I am still no closer to finding Kristi's mountain. It has been seven years since she left us; at times I think it is time to end the search. Yet, I continue to believe I will find it one day.

I have an opportunity to go to Peru on a tour with Gregg Braden. Gregg is one of my favorite teachers and the thought of traveling in Peru and experiencing all the mystic sites is tantalizing.

I look at the photos of Machu Picchu, lush and green peaking through the mist. It is a magical land of ancient pyramids, numinous temples of forgotten rituals and hidden portals; once a gateway to the galaxies, from which gods and messengers would freely pass, it now lies sleeping, quietly guarding its secrets until humanity is ready to receive its wisdom once again.

I am convinced this is the mountain Kristi has been referring to. I feel as if this is my last chance to connect with her.

For months I work to make it happen. I visualize and even create a vision board. I save my money and plan my trip. I imagine what it would be like to really see Kristi again.

"Is this the mountain I am to meet you at, Kristi? If it is, please help me make this trip a reality."

Turns out, Peru and Machu Picchu were not to be.

I am devastated. Did I miss my window to meet you Kristi?

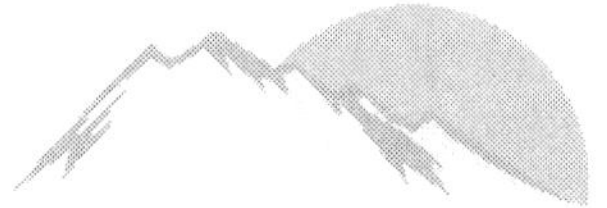

CHAPTER 22

Let Go of Your Story

"I've been burdened with blame
trapped in the past for too long,
I'm moving on."
~ Rascal Flatts

My life has evolved much over the past seven years. I have learned a great deal from these amazing teachers I have been blessed to work with. I am more aware of the messages from my guides and angels, welcoming their input and support. I have a better understanding of the concept that we are all energy and that by raising our frequency, the ability to connect with Source, Spirit, the Universe, God—whatever you want to call the Divine power that created us, is possible for us all.

I am once again on my bike. It is relaxing riding the trails in quiet solitude, mindful only of the breeze blowing gently through the trees. I stop at a small pond and sit on the shore to contemplate and connect with my guides and angels. There is not a living being in sight. No person, bird, animal, or fish is visible. Just me.

"Let go of your story, Donna," my guides say. "Let go of your story about Kristi, about who you are. It is time."

I realize I am so much more than just a mother who lost a child. Yes, that is a part of who I am, but it does not define me, any more than my business does. Each is a part of the fabric of my life, a grand quilt made of many different threads. Yet I am so much more than that. I am Donna, a spiritual being, a unique expression of God with a Divine purpose.

For the first time since sitting down I notice movement, a small snake swimming through the water in front of me. How appropriate; the snake has long been a symbol of death and rebirth, shedding its skin as it outgrows the old. I am reminded of a quote by one of my favorite teachers, don Miguel Ruiz:

"Whatever life takes away from you, let it go. When you surrender and let go of the past, you allow yourself to be fully alive in the moment. Letting go of the past means you can enjoy the dream that is happening right now."

Too often we hang onto our story for dear life—the anger and resentment, sadness and guilt. We become attached to our story; we have a picture in our mind of who we think we are, unable to envision that we are anything else than what our past circumstances have made us. Our picture of the world and ourselves is colored and distorted by the things that have happened to us. And we accept that to be true.

What if there is another life, just waiting for us to open the door? The Universe hates a vacuum. Sometimes all it takes is letting go of the old for the new to come forth. In reality, we are afraid that if we let our story go we won't know who we are anymore. Our story becomes us and heaven help anyone who tries to shake it loose. Author and speaker Caroline Myss brought that message home perfectly one night while speaking at a BellaSpark event in Fort Collins. She has a tendency to tell it like it is, and she doesn't mince words.

"So you had a bad childhood? Get over it!" she loudly declared to the audience. Boy, did she push some buttons that night.

The truth is we give our power away to our story, to the one who wronged us, hurt us, left us. This becomes our prison, keeping us from stepping out into our true light: the divine person we came here to be. The greatest gift we can give ourselves is forgiveness, both for the person or thing that hurt us and for ourselves. It will set us free.

Each of us has a choice in how to live our life. We can choose to live with fear and anger or we can choose love and gratitude. We can wallow in our story, filled with past hurts and resentments, or we can focus on creating a new story, one that highlights our grandest vision for ourselves: a life of passion and joy.

I spend an entire year producing events with Dr. Joe Dispenza. In his workshops, Dr. Joe demonstrates how old beliefs and buried emotions are often the driving force behind our thoughts and actions, directing us unconsciously as we continuously play out old patterns and scenarios over and over. Good or bad, big or small, these emotions lie deeply hidden, smoldering beneath the surface. We might not even know what is causing us to respond a certain way—perhaps an incident on the playground when we were seven that made us feel insecure, a rebuke or scolding from a parent, a betrayal from someone we trusted; there are many things we bury inside. They're in there, just waiting to show up in physical form as disease and pain, or anger, addiction, lack, and depression. And while I won't try to explain the science behind how the brain works, it is clear to me that much of what we do, say, and think, as well as how we respond and react is based on old patterns, habits, and beliefs. Our brain has been conditioned to respond in a certain way when it is confronted with a specific occurrence and it will continue to react the same way until we release the emotion or change the belief.

Through deep meditation practice we learn how to release these old emotions and beliefs in order to change the way the brain responds. In effect, we are able to rewire our brain to create the outcome we desire, rather than continue to operate from the past.

This weekend is one of Dr. Joe's advanced workshops; over one hundred people are in attendance. Incredible things can happen when you bring large groups together with a similar intention. The energies of multiple people all meditating at the same time greatly expand the capacity to connect to a higher power. Miraculous healings and emotional shifts can occur.

Dr. Joe is leading us through a deep meditation, once again focusing our attention on releasing a desired belief or emotion. I have had various experiences during these meditations. Sometimes I sense a rush of powerful energy; other times it feels as if I am in some sort of dream state. Today is different. I am sitting straight in my chair, feet on the floor, palms face up in my lap, eyes closed. In my mind's eye I see Kristi kneeling on the floor in front of me, her hands are circling my cheeks. Behind her are my guides David, Zura, my big blue angel, and Jesus. Kristi smiles as she reaches into my chest and pulls out a large smoldering lump of black coal. She holds it in front of me for a minute before passing it to David, who passes it to Zura, who passes it to my angel, who then passes it to Jesus. Jesus holds the still-smoldering lump of coal in his hands, and then closing his palms around it, rubs his hands together. He opens his hands to reveal what is now a mound of thick black coal dust. With one deep breath, he blows it away.

Chapter 23
Last Holiday

"Next time . . . we will laugh more,
we'll love more; we just won't be so afraid."
~ Georgia Byrd, *Last Holiday*

I have just completed two more weekends with Dr. Joe Dispenza, one in Seattle and the second in Vancouver. They have been powerful workshops with a concentrated emphasis on meditating and again releasing old beliefs. My focus has been on shifting my subconscious ideas around abundance and worthiness; it has been an intense couple of weeks. I know my big dreams for myself and BellaSpark will never be realized until I can move past old patterns that hold me back.

Somehow I have come down with a cold, coughing and sneezing, barely able to talk, and by Saturday I have lost my voice completely. I am tired and sick. Not only that but it has been raining the entire time I have been in the Pacific Northwest and I am desperate for some sunshine. I just want to go home. Driving my rental car back to the Seattle airport from Vancouver early Sunday morning, my goal is to see if I can catch an earlier plane home to Colorado.

Unfortunately, given the current state of the airline industry, all Frontier flights to Denver are full. How I miss the days when planes were only partially full and we weren't crammed into the seats like cattle. I have spent the last ten days coordinating the logistics for a couple hundred people and bunking with others, first with my sister and then my Vancouver partner, Karen. The thought of spending another night with more people, albeit family, is disconcerting. I decide to find a nice hotel close to the airport; I will fly home in the morning as planned. I envision a hotel with a nice restaurant and a hot tub, a really good dinner and glass of wine. It is already calling me. My thoughts go to the Seattle Marriott I had scouted out earlier in the week for another upcoming event. It is less than a mile from the airport and has a beautiful atrium complete with a hot tub and an upscale restaurant with an extensive wine list—it is the perfect spot for a quiet night. However, the Marriott is expensive and right away my mind goes to the extra cost. There surely is another hotel in the vicinity with nice amenities, perhaps more reasonably priced. I am feeling guilty for even considering such an extravagance.

The rain is coming down in buckets now, the sky getting darker and gloomier by the minute. I pull into a parking spot at a nearby mall and proceed to search for a hotel on my phone. I am certainly not adept at surfing the net with my phone; the knowledge and skill needed to manipulate this new technology having skipped over me when first introduced. I plug in the requirements I want and peruse the Hotels.com site only to hit a wrong button, lose everything and have to start all over again—a frustrating occurrence that happens numerous times. I look at locations and photos, trying to determine if this hotel or that one might have what I am looking for. In the back of my mind there is a tiny a hint that instead of relaxing in a cozy room I am spending my afternoon sitting in my car in the rain, but in the illness-induced fog my brain does not compute. *Is the Universe toying with me?*

Almost two hours pass before I finally find what looks like a good deal. The hotel has a pool and hot tub and a restaurant/bar. The pictures on the website seem pretty nice, and the price is great. Desperate to get settled, I book it knowing it is non-refundable.

I certainly get what I paid for. The lobby is almost non-existent, the room small and noisy, and to add insult to insult, the restaurant is closed on Sundays. I argue with the poor girl at the front desk, but it is obvious she can't do anything for me. Wet and cold and feeling sicker by the moment, I resign myself to my folly. Gone is my relaxing evening and my glass of good wine.

Having not eaten since early that morning, I get back in my car in the now-pouring rain to search for some food. As luck would have it, there is nothing in the area but a few fast food restaurants. I settle on a Pizza Hut several blocks away, order a pizza and Coke to go and drive back to my hotel with dinner. Not only do I feel awful but my nice meal is reduced to take-out pizza eaten on the bed in my dingy hotel room. That is what I get for wanting to be thrifty. I hope that maybe there is at least something on the television; I find a movie, hoping it will bring a little brightness to this disaster.

The movie is *Last Holiday* starring Queen Latifah. It is the story of a woman who is told by her doctor that she has just a few weeks to live. Having toed the line her entire life while living frugally and denying herself the things she wants to see and do, she decides to cash in her retirement and for once live the life of her dreams, if only for a few short weeks. She flies to Europe first class, stays at the hotel she has been fantasizing about for years, enjoys massages and spa days, learns to snowboard, and cooks with the hotel's famous chef she has idolized. She experiences all the things she had dreamed of doing but never allowed for herself. One of the best lines is "Next time . . . we will laugh more, we'll love more; we just won't be so afraid." Of course there is a happy ending: the diagnosis is wrong and Queen Latifah is not dying. She goes on to do all the things she had wanted for her life.

I love *Last Holiday*, and believe me, the message hits home as I sit on the bed eating pizza. I have spent the previous two weekends learning to release my beliefs that I don't deserve nice things, that I am not good enough to have that which I desire, that abundance is not attainable for me. Thank you Spirit for putting it right in front of my face so I can't miss it! I do deserve to have what I desire. Abundance is my birthright. It is true for all of us.

It is two weeks later and I am again on the road, this time heading to Portland, Oregon. Interestingly, when I check my itinerary I discover I have somehow scheduled my flight to come in a day early. Don't ask me how; I am pretty diligent about schedules and live by the calendar, but here I am in Portland a day ahead of time with nothing to do. The workshop I am producing is in a terrific hotel in the downtown area; it has a really nice restaurant/bar. With nothing to prepare, I spend the afternoon wandering around the city enjoying the Japanese Garden, the little shops and the sights, more carefree than I have been in months. Dinner is spectacular: oysters Rockefeller, medium rare steak cooked just perfectly along with a fresh green salad, crème brûlée for dessert, and of course a glass of my favorite wine. I do not feel one bit guilty!

I have almost given up hope.

I have been searching for this mountain for eight years now.

I have yet to find it.

I couldn't have made it up; Kimmie gave me your message twice.

You told her you will meet me at the base of the mountain.

I trust her; I truly believe it was a message from you.

What does it mean Kristi?

Chapter 24
Moonie

"A sister is a gift to the heart, a friend to the spirit, a golden thread to the meaning of life."
~ Isadora James

It is mid-December and I am taking my grandson Drew to lunch. We are headed downtown to see the Christmas displays and perhaps have a visit with Santa. Chatting about school and hockey, his favorite sport, we are interrupted by the ringing of my cell phone.

"Yeow!" he squeals, getting a kick out of my ring tone. We are laughing.

"It's Moonie," I say, glancing at the caller ID. Moonie is our favorite nickname for my sister Mary. "Hi Moonie." But the woman's voice on the other end is not my sister's.

"Is this Donna? I am supposed to call Donna. There's something wrong with your sister; we called the ambulance."

"Where are you?" I ask, frantically turning the car around. She describes a shopping center about twenty minutes away. And then the voice on the other end of the line is gone.

It is snowy and the roads are slick. I drive like a bat out of hell, silently praying to my angels to please give me all green lights and no speeding tickets. Help me find this place.

Drew and I arrive at the location the woman gave us. There is no ambulance in sight and no one around who can fill us in, only Moonie's little red car parked not far away. They must have taken her to the hospital just up the street.

We find Moonie in the emergency room alone, a flurry of hospital staff hustling in and out of her room, trying to stabilize her, running tests.

"She has a ruptured aortic aneurysm. We have to operate immediately. Her blood pressure is down to 60. Are you her next of kin? Can you sign for her?"

Moonie is semi-coherent and in a lot of pain but I think maybe, for a just a moment, she recognizes me.

"Take care of my babies," she pleads, referring to her three cats. And then she is rolled through a set of big double doors. It is the last time we talk.

Joined in the waiting room by my husband, my children and my grandchildren, we sit somberly, the atmosphere thick with worry. My sister never married nor had any children of her own. She was a second mother to my children, and of course my grandchildren were special to her, loving them perhaps more unconditionally than I could. My son Adam's wife Jen works at the hospital and has access to areas that we are not privy to. She periodically goes behind closed doors and brings back information. We wait in silence.

Finally, the doctor comes out. He looks tired; the surgery was extensive, over six hours.

"Well," he says. "Your sister made it through the surgery. Now we wait and see if she makes it through the night."

The vigil continues. My brother and sisters have been called. They are on their way.

Turns out, Moonie is remarkably strong; her body is stabilizing.

"She should start waking up in another day or two," they tell us.

We continue to wait. Word has gotten out to Moonie's friends. A steady stream of visitors shows up at the ICU; she is constantly surrounded by those who love her. It's almost as if Moonie is holding court as they chat with her, encourage her to wake up. Silently, she lays in her bed, slightly propped up with pillows, eyes closed, listening but not responding; it is a one-sided conversation. *Wake up Moonie. Wake up!*

How did she get the name Moonie? Actually, her given name is Mary; bestowed upon her after the misfortune of being born on Christmas Day. My son Jason, just learning to talk, could not say Mary. He called her Moonie and, like all crazy nicknames, it stuck. When Moonie moved to Colorado to be closer to us she decided to change her name to Marnie— a new place, a new name, a new start, a chance to be someone other than who she was. The poor hospital staff is totally confused. My family calls her Moonie, my brother and sisters call her Mary and when her friends show up they ask for Marnie.

It has been a couple days now since Moonie first entered the hospital. I am spending my time by her side, returning home late at night to grab a few hours sleep before heading back to keep vigil. Tonight, for the first time in months, I dream. I rarely remember my dreams, usually waking up grasping at a glimpse of something I can't quite put my finger on. But tonight the dream is so vivid I can't get it out of my mind, replaying over and over like a song stuck in one's head, only this time with pictures.

Moonie is with me, only she is a small child. "What are you doing here, Moonie?" I ask. "We have to get you back to the hospital." I wrap my sister in a blanket and gently put her in the car. Frantically I drive this way and that. I am thwarted everywhere I go—trains crashing, roads ending, wrong turns, arriving at a destination only to find it is not the hospital.

"Can you give me directions to the hospital?" I stop everyone I meet, pleading with them. "I have to get my sister back to the hospital. Please help me. I don't know what to do." I am desperate, tears running down my face.

A week goes by. Her body is responding, but Moonie is not. The staff runs tests and then more tests. We learn that she suffered serious brain damage, most likely when her blood pressure dropped so dangerously. Even if she does wake up, she will be severely paralyzed and incapacitated. I am once again alone. My brother and sisters return home, back to their jobs, their lives.

"We trust you to make the right decision," they tell me as they drive off. "We love you."

I meet with all of her doctors: the heart surgeon, the internist, the neurologist. One by one they tell me their opinion, skirting around the one question on my mind. Only one has the courage to say what he thinks.

"If she were my sister, I would let her go," he says.

What do you want me to do Moonie? Are you ready to go home? The choice is yours. Please don't make me be the one to decide.

I look at death so differently now since Kristi died. I know without a doubt that the soul lives on. I believe that we can connect with those we love who have passed. I am fortunate to be supported by amazing friends, intuitives, and psychics who know how to connect. They tell me Moonie is enjoying being out of her heavy, pain-ridden body and she is deciding. The choice is hers, they remind me. She will choose whether to stay or go.

Moonie, you are such a beautiful soul. Why do you doubt your lovability? Why is life such a struggle for you? Are you really ready?

I know she is tired, as am I. Life can be hard; I wonder what it would feel like to finally go Home. I sign the papers to disconnect the breathing tube.

It's up to you now, Moonie. I trust you will choose the right path for yourself. I will be with you.

Again, her strength astounds me. For a time, she has chosen to stay. I am at the hospital continuously now, leaving only for short periods to clean up and change clothes. Jenny keeps watch when I am away. She has a special bond with this woman, and we know Moonie does not want to be alone. I am most grateful for the nights when all is quiet. No nervous small talk with other family members or the continuous stream of visitors. No hospital staff constantly checking vitals. I like the quiet, just us. Sometimes I sit silently, holding her hand. Often, I talk and she listens. I tell stories of when we were children, reminding her of the good times. I am given a small book, *Finding Stone* by Cristin Lore Weber. It is a beautiful story of life and death; I realize that just as a stone is honed and polished by the river so is our soul by life. I stay up all night reading it out loud, my voice the only thing piercing the eerie stillness of the sleeping hospital. I am reading it for Moonie, but know the message is really for me.

Kristi is with us, and perhaps others—angels, guides, our parents; I am not sure. I still don't have the gift of sight but I feel them. Sometimes, as I keep my silent vigil in the middle of the night, the motion-activated paper towel machine will start spitting out towels.

"Who's here?" I ask.

I remind Moonie that it is ok if she is ready to move on. She will be happy.

It is now ten days since this journey began. I am dozing on the sofa next to Moonie. It is late and the hospital is once again quiet when I hear the voice.

"Donna. Wake up!" The voice is loud and insistent. Startled, I jump up.

I'm awake.

I look at my sister as she takes one last deep breath; she is at peace.

A Tribute to My Sister

You were a Christmas baby, born on December 25, hence the name Mary. Compassionate, caring, generous, and loving, you embodied Christmas year-round, sharing your many beautiful gifts with all. You loved to make unique presents for family and friends, but your true gift, the one you gave so freely, was your heart.

You were my big sister. We shared a bed when we were children, snuggling together, whispering in the dark. Interesting how life always brings us full circle. I lay next to you those last few nights, sharing stories of our childhood. And I read to you, just as I did when we were children, me just learning to read, you helping me sound out the words. This time you were quiet, but I knew you were listening. It was a beautiful book, a parable about the journey of life; you understood far better than I.

Having had no children of your own, you embraced first my children and then my grandchildren. They called you Moonie and you were a wonderful aunt, always there for them, providing a safe, fun-filled space for them to just be, exactly and only who they were. Your gift of unconditional love helped to mold them into the wonderful people they grew to be.

When my daughter Kristi died, you were the first one there, making the phone calls, helping us navigate the thorny path of grief and loss. You were strong, a rock I could lean on, even though your own heart was breaking.

You had a steady stream of visitors at the hospital, testament to the many people you shared your light with. Like most of us, I don't think you realized how many people you touched, how many peo-

ple loved you. I could tell you were enjoying the attention, basking in the love of family and friends. I called you Queen Moonie, holding court one last time and you graced us with one beautiful final gift, the chance to say goodbye.

Thank you Moonie, for allowing me to be with you as you took your last breath. I have been blessed by you, first in life and then in death. You gave me the most precious gift of all. Peace and joy be with you until we are together again.

I love you.

Chapter 25
Out of the Mouths of Babes

"While we try to teach our children all about life... our children teach us what life is all about."
- Angela Schwindt

My family had never been one to believe in angels or ghosts or the ability to see or talk to loved ones who passed on, before Kristi died. We didn't disbelieve either; it just wasn't part of our arena. After all, most people don't really talk about meeting angels or having conversations or encounters with dead people. What a wonderful relief it was for me to connect to a psychic medium and know that Kristi was okay. Of course, that's what mediums do; they have special abilities that the average person doesn't possess, gifts that allow them to have contact with the other side. However, it wasn't a medium that ultimately convinced me this was possible for all of us. What really opened my eyes was my grandchildren's ability to see and talk to their Auntie Kristi and then Auntie Moonie after she died.

My oldest grandson, Nick, was six when Kristi died; they were buddies. After her death, he would share with us that Kristi often popped into his room to say hi and visit. We talked about these happenings occasionally; I wanted him to be comfortable with these occurrences and not think it was weird or out of the ordinary. At age nine, Nick would walk home from school and be alone for a short time until his dad got back from work. Driving Nick home one afternoon, I asked if he had seen Kristi lately.

"She sits on the couch with me after school until my dad gets home," he replied.

How nice that he knew he was not really alone, that he always had someone keeping him company. Later that spring, I asked if Kristi still sat with him after school.

"Yes. But sometimes I think I see her at school. And sometimes when I'm having trouble with my math, she whispers the answer in my ear. *Twenty-five,*" he whispered.

Bob and I laughed. *This could be trouble, Kristi was terrible at math!*

My grandson Drew, who was just a few months old when Kristi passed, often described various encounters with Kristi. She would appear in his room in the middle of the night, and the two would play until all hours of the morning, much to the frustration of his mother when he was difficult to get up the next day.

My granddaughter Hampton also saw Kristi from the time she was small. After all, growing up with two older cousins who automatically included Kristi in their play, it came naturally to her.

Often, while playing in the backyard, one of the kids would pop in to report. "Kristi's here. She's sitting up in the tree watching us." Sometimes they would tell me she was sitting in the back seat of the car between them as we headed out on excursion. I think she likes being around them, their spontaneity, their innocence and their loving energy.

Children are so wonderfully open; it's no surprise they can still connect with the heavens. My grandchildren and I share stories about angels and spirits all the time; all three are amazingly gifted and able to tune into the higher frequencies with ease. One night, while lying in bed next to Drew trying to get him to settle down and go to sleep, I asked if he could see angels. He told me about his angels and how they are around all the time, especially at night.

"Do you see my angel?" I asked.

He raised his head up and slowly gazed toward the ceiling.

"Wow, he's really tall!" he exclaimed.

A new generation of children is being born, and they are gifted in many ways and forms. No matter the terms used to describe them: Indigo Children, Crystal Kids, Rainbow, Psychic, Super Psychic or others, the overall meaning is the same. They are intuitive, spiritually gifted, and aware.

According to Doreen Virtue, who has studied these new children over the years, Indigos have a warrior spirit with strong tempers and fiery determination, making it difficult to conform to the dysfunctional systems they encounter at home, work, or school. Their collective purpose is to mash down old structures that no longer serve us. Kristi definitely was an Indigo.

Crystal children began to appear on the planet from about 1990 to 2010. These children are among the most connected, communicative, and caring. Crystal children are the way of the new world, and they bring to us a level of kindness and sensitivity we have never experienced. Crystal children use their telepathic abilities from the moment they appear on this planet. These children are extremely powerful; their main purpose is to take us to the next level in our evolution and reveal to us our inner power and divinity.

Both the Indigo and Crystal children/adults are here to assist the world as we evolve to a higher vibration where love and empathy become the norm rather than the exception. It is important that we recognize them and support them. I see these traits in my grandchildren.

It has been a little over three months since Moonie left us. I am babysitting my eight-year-old granddaughter Hampton. With plans to spend the night even though she tosses and turns like a wild cat barely leaving me room to lie down, much less get any slumber, I agree to sleep in her bed with her. We wake in the morning to a quiet house, content to snuggle and enjoy our time together.

"Nana, do you want to play I Spy?" Hampton asks. I Spy With My Little Eye is a favorite game between my grandchildren and me. She pauses. "Moonie plays I Spy with me all the time."

"When did you see Moonie?" I am surprised.

"She sleeps with me every night."

I want to know more. I know my grandchildren have connected with Kristi. I am delighted to learn that Moonie has been able to reach across the veils also.

"How is she doing?" I ask.

"Really well; she's not in pain any more," Hampton tells me.

"How does she look?"

"She looks just like that picture at the funeral; the one where she was cooking in the kitchen."

Moonie had struggled with weight her entire life. There was a time though, when she was very slim and trim. We had several photos from that period on display at the funeral. The picture Hampton is referring to is one of those.

"She can also be in more than one place at a time," Hampton goes on to explain. "She can be with me and Drew at the same time."

I am happy that Hampton has her favorite great aunt with her all the time. What a gift Moonie has given her.

Several weeks later. Hampton and I are having our favorite lunch, pizza, at the Pizza Hut in Target. It is our tradition; first we go shopping and then we sit on the stools by the window watching the people go by, enjoying our pizza and talking about the important things in the life of a eight-year-old. That day we have company.

"Kristi and Moonie are sitting with us," Hampton offers. "Kristi is having pizza and Moonie is eating a corndog."

Of course she is. Corndogs were Moonie's favorite.

"They can't stay very long. They are going shopping. Moonie needs some new clothes; size extra small."

I smile. Moonie is so proud of her new shape.

It is spring; almost five months have passed since Moonie left us. Hampton and I are enjoying another of our preferred pastimes, bowling. I don't know if the bumpers blocking the gutters are for Hampton or more for my sake, but it sure helps our game! We are in the ninth frame and Hampton throws one of her best balls of the day. Nine pins go down. *Dang, it should have been a strike.* She is determined to get a spare, but that single pin on the far right corner is difficult to hit. She carefully throws the ball, trying hard to lay it down the far right side of the alley, but unfortunately, it is making a big curve to the left; there is no way she will hit that last pin. And then the craziest thing happens—all of a sudden the ball takes a sharp turn to the right, and down goes the pin.

"Hampton, did you see that?" I exclaim.

She is laughing. "Moonie and Kristi were sneaking down there and pushed the ball over. I told them, 'You don't have to sneak; no one else can see you!'"

This time Hampton and I are enjoying lunch with my grandson Drew. At age eleven, he is more like a big brother to her than a cousin. They love to spend time together. We are sitting in a booth with the two kids on one side and me on the other. The music coming from the sound system is country and western.

"Can you see that, Hampton?" Drew is laughing. "Kristi and Moonie are dancing a Hoedown!"

I turn around to look over my shoulder, but of course, I see nothing. Hampton starts to laugh as well, both kids enjoying their aunts' crazy antics.

"Moonie is wearing a handlebar moustache," Drew tells me. He shows me how she is stroking it, curling the ends up, making funny faces. "Can't you see them Nana?" he says. "They're right here!"

For them, seeing is so natural; it is like looking at you or me. I ask Drew what it looks like when he sees Moonie, Kristi, Papa Joe (his great-grandfather with whom he had a special bond) and angels. He describes it like this:

"They have a black outline around them and a grey shadow behind them. But inside the outline, they look real, and they wear real clothes. Papa Joe always wears a white sleeveless t-shirt and army khakis like he does in the picture we have of him when he was young and in the army. He plays soldier with me a lot.

Moonie is younger and skinny, maybe 35 years old. And Kristi looks the same as she does in the pictures I see of her.

Angels show up the same, except they wear bathrobes, and I can see their wings. And when they touch me, it feels like a soft feather across my skin."

Hampton and my oldest grandson, Nick, also describe their seeing in much the same way. Spirits are in full color, though sometimes a little hazy, more opaque than a live person. Angels have wings and typically wear a solid color, though the color may vary.

I am grateful that my grandchildren have this wonderful ability to see and connect with my daughter and my sister. My sister spends more time with them now then she was able to when alive. After all, she can be in more than one place at a time (smile). I know that they are guided and protected by Kristi and Moonie and I am grateful that I have them to show me and remind me that they are with us always.

I have to admit though, sometimes I am jealous. Why is it I cannot see like them? For them it is effortless, for me a struggle. They see spirits and other beings in front of them through their normal two eyes. I tend to see things more in my mind's eye, inside my head. It is more remote and less vivid, almost like watching a movie, not usually interactive. It doesn't feel quite real.

What a precious gift, to know without a doubt that my grandchildren are not alone, that they can connect to their loved ones and angels whenever they want. We, too, can have that gift. The abilities to see, hear, feel, and connect with those on the other side—including our loved ones, guides, and angels—are available to all of us. We just have to uncover them and learn how to utilize them. I am still practicing, with the help of my grandchildren.

CHAPTER 26

A Message from the Other Side

"Death—the last sleep?
No, it is the final awakening."
- Walter Scott

Moonie came to me with a message recently. I still don't see her like my grandchildren do, but I am now able to hear her. I asked her what it was like when she was in a coma, when she died. This is what she had to say:

At first I didn't know where I was. I knew I was no longer in my body, everything felt so light, weightless. It felt good to be out of that heavy form, no pain, either physical or emotional. I was floating in some sort of heavy fog, very dense and I couldn't see much else. Confusing, on the one hand scary, on the other a feeling of being neutral, neither joy nor sadness. I could see you and all of my family and friends, sitting with me, holding my hand. I could feel your love for me and knew you wanted me to wake up, but I was so tired. Life had been so hard for me. I realize now that I didn't love myself and so I created walls around me to prevent others' love from touching me.

I was floating in a sort of no-man's land, feeling disconnected and very much alone. I didn't know what to do. Somehow, in all that fog I came to think of your friend Anne. Not sure if she reached out to me or I reached out to her, but all of a sudden I found myself at her home. It was morning and she was showering. Someone knocked over something on her counter to catch her attention. Perhaps it was me but more likely one of my guides or Kristi trying to help me. The noise made Anne aware someone was there and that's when she must have realized it was me. Anne got out of the shower and wrapping up in a bath robe, invited me to sit next to her on the bed. She knew I was lost and anxious. I remember asking her, probably telepathically, I wasn't sure at the time, "Where am I? I don't know what to do."

She told me I was in between. Then she said, "Look up, Moonie. Look up!" That's when I could see the light, like sunlight breaking through the fog. I realized I was surrounded by angels and guides; yes, Kristi was there, and even Mom and Dad. The next thing I knew the fog was gone and I, too, was in the light, surrounded by these loving beings. It was a feeling I had forgotten while in my body, such beautiful unconditional love. It was indescribable. Please thank Anne for opening the door for me.

Turns out I wasn't done yet with the lessons I had come to earth to learn this lifetime. Truth be told, I wasn't sure I wanted to come back. I was weary of the life I had created. While my physical body was lying in the hospital, my soul was meeting with my guides determining my course of action. I could return to the physical world and complete the lessons I had planned, or I could return home to learn those lessons on this side. We all come in with contracts and lessons, things we agree to experience when we incarnate, all designed for our soul's evolution. I had not yet completed mine. My guides and I agreed that going back would be difficult given the condition of my body and that it would be a wiser course of action to exit now. I will be able to return again, hopefully from a better perspective and continue my soul's journey.

I did visit Anne one last time, after I made my transition. She described it to you as me jumping up and down saying "I did it. I did it!" I have to admit, I was pretty excited. I was really ready to make my transition and return Home. It is so beautiful here sometimes I am amazed any of us wants to leave. Yet there is something special about the earth plane, unlike anywhere else in the universe. A soul can experience so much in just one lifetime; it's a more accelerated learning and can facilitate our evolution and growth much quicker. I know it seems difficult to comprehend, but time is not measured in the same linear fashion here. What feels like years and decades to you, from this side of the veil time spent on earth passes in the blink of an eye.

I love you Donna and am grateful for all you brought to my life. Thank you for being my sister and for being with me as I made my transition. I will be with you always.

- Moonie

CHAPTER 27

A Change of Cosmic Address

"Death is one of two things . . . Either it is annihilation,
and the dead have no consciousness of anything;
or, as we are told,
it is really a change: a migration
of the soul from one place to another."
~ Socrates

As I mentioned, I look at death differently now. I have experienced the death of six people who were close to me, five in the last ten years. My father, my daughter, my mother, my husband's parents and finally my sister all left this earth to move on. I know there will be more over the course of my lifetime. It is a fact of life that we all leave this world at some time. I now use the word transition, for though our body may cease to be, our soul lives on, transitioning from this physical plane back to the heavenly dimension from which it came. Our souls never die, they simply return Home to the infinite Source of all life.

And yes, for those left behind, the pain can be overwhelming.

We miss our loved ones when they move on. We miss the physical aspect of them, touching them, interacting with them. More than anything though, it really boils down to missing the connection we have with Spirit and losing a loved one seems to amplify that feeling of disconnect, of separation. The good news is we can still connect with them, now more easily then ever, as the veils are being lifted between this dimension and others. My granddaughter Hampton spends more time now with her Auntie Moonie than she ever did when Moonie was alive. I, too, find it is getting easier to tune in and connect to my sister and my daughter. They are both just a thought away.

I am reminded of an interview with actor Terrance Stamp on NPR radio. In the course of the conversation the topic of death came up. Stamp beautifully described death as *a change of cosmic address*. What a wonderful perspective.

Sarina Baptista, a gifted psychic medium, is quick to reassure us that our loved ones are available to talk to us whenever we ask, even if they now abide in a different location. She describes it as a doorbell ringing, signaling our loved ones that someone wants to visit. They respond immediately; our only job to step through the door and be receptive to the messages they send. I can easily imagine the Universe made up of many houses, each one in a different dimension and frequency. We live in the 3rd dimension house and thus we have a 3D address; our loved ones who have transitioned live in another dimension, perhaps the 7th or 8th. They now have a 7D or 8D address. Just as we might visit a family member who has moved to a new address, ringing their doorbell when we arrive, so, too, can we connect with those on the other side, ringing their doorbell, letting them know we are there ready to visit. I ring my loved ones' doorbells often, and when they open the door, delight in spending some time with them.

Where are you Kristi?

Where is the mountain?

Is it in the United States?

Somewhere on the other side of the planet?

I know you talk to me; I can hear your words in my head.

I feel you guiding me often, but you have yet to tell me where the mountain is.

Nine years is a long time.

It seems as if I have been searching forever.

There is so much I don't understand, so much I have yet to learn.

I am trying Kristi, but at times I feel so lost.

CHAPTER 28

Lose Sight of the Shore

"You can never cross the ocean unless you have the courage to lose sight of the shore."
- Christopher Columbus

I feel as if I have been set adrift without a paddle. Tossed into a boat on a raging ocean without so much as a life jacket to keep me from drowning; no means to reach the nearest shore, even if I can see it. I am weary of this spiritual path. The world does not seem to understand this new perspective and frankly I don't either.

I question the choices I have made. I plead with my guides to show me that the last nine years I have been on this journey haven't been for naught. I am no longer sure that my path is the right one; that the events and programs I create are what I am to do. Once I was so sure of my vision, now I am sure of nothing.

Perhaps I am the crazy one. Am I imagining all this woo-woo spiritual stuff? Why does it not make sense? Where is it all going? Or more importantly, where am I going?

Am I a fool? I am pretty sure my family thinks I am. I have just returned from spending the weekend with my family—the successful business people who seem to have it all figured out. I am sure they all think I am crazy. Maybe I am. None of this seems to make sense any more. This global shift we are supposedly in, maybe it's just one of those cycles humanity goes through, nothing special or spiritual about it. I know nothing any more. At times I feel so alone. The large circle of friends I once had has gotten smaller and smaller, and though I am supported by a group of amazing souls who understand this spiritual arena, I feel lost at times. Alone once again—why am I surprised?

Why me? Why did this have to happen to me? Why did Kristi have to die? What is the purpose? I have asked these questions a million times and though my heart knows the answer, my brain still struggles to wrap itself around it. The concept that I chose this existence is at times still difficult to accept. Why would I choose to lose my daughter? Why would I choose this life and all the challenges? I am so weary. *I surrender, God. Show me the way.*

My answer comes from a guide by the name of Solomon in the book *Solomon Speaks* by Eric Pearl and Frederick Ponzlov:

> *Trials make us stronger. . . . This life is not*
> *meant necessarily to be easy, because if it were easy,*
> *there would be nothing to grow from. I'm not*
> *saying that you're going to suffer. You're not here*
> *to suffer; you're put here to enjoy. But it's the*
> *process of learning how to enjoy that's important –*
> *that you do not become a victim to an event,*
> *but derive joy from it, whatever the event may be.*

My father's death laid the groundwork, but it was Kristi's leaving that was the catalyst for my journey and my transformation from a life of shadow to one of light. I know now that until I felt the depths of grief, I could never really understand the pain others go through. I could not have the insight to recognize without a doubt that life goes on. I know that we are more than our physical bodies, that we are infinite souls and when we leave this earthly realm we return to that which we came. I know that the Universe and our loved ones are around us all the time, supporting and loving us, even though most of us cannot see or hear them with our human senses.

We are indeed infinite spiritual beings having a physical experience, the earth nothing more than a highly developed school. We choose our parents, our children, our sex, our race, our nationality, and more. We also choose the lessons we wish to learn in this lifetime. Then once we return to the infinite Universe, when ready, we do it all over again. We decide to learn and experience something new, because it is our soul's desire to continue to explore and evolve.

Linda Star Wolfe, a guest on my radio show *InnerViews with Kimmie Rose and Donna Visocky*, described the challenges we go through during our lifetime as initiations of the soul. Often those facing the biggest initiations have come to this world to learn lessons about death, rebirth, and transformation. If that's the case, I must have signed up for the advanced course!

Despite these tests, if we can change our perspective from one of challenges, problems, or tragedies and look at life from a higher perspective, we might see the blessing in all that has happened to us. When we ask what our soul might have wanted to learn from these events, often the message is clear, though we may not like it. We can succumb to the anger and grief or we can embrace all that the lesson has taught us and find joy in living. Wolfe affirms this earth plane is a school and " . . . it is by far the best place in the entire universe to earn a PhD in Spirituality."

Yes we may still get bounced around; the waves of the ocean can be furious at times. Yet I know that we are never alone. We can call on our angels; they will support us and guide us to smoother waters.

Kristi said, "We agreed to do this." At times I still question that choice, but when I look back on my life I can see the path this experience has led me on—the lessons (fun and not so fun) I have learned, and the people who have been my teachers on this journey. I see the perfection of the divine plan. My grief and loss have led me to a purpose I could never have known, to places of unimaginable beauty and peace. Life is a gift we have been given, for only in this world can we experience so very much—love and hate, joy and sadness, darkness and light. It can be an amazing voyage if we choose to look at it that way. Time to let go of the shore and ride the waves, set sail for distant lands ripe with exciting adventures. I am looking forward to the next leg of this journey.

CHAPTER 29

The Pie Plate

"Nothing has any power over me other than that which I give it through my conscious thoughts."
- Anthony Robbins

One of the keys to stepping into this new reality, to raising our vibration and truly connecting to Spirit, is being present. The past is gone and the future not yet here. All we really have is this moment. When we live in the present we are capable of creating amazing things, a future we want, a life that matches our desires and dreams. Unfortunately, we tend to look at life linearly, a continuous and ongoing line documenting our past, present, and future. Too often we base how we react to something in the present on events that have occurred in our past, and then again use that past as the template for creating our future, thus history repeats itself. Albert Einstein describes insanity as "...doing the same thing over and over again and expecting different results." We have become insane experts.

Much of what we do throughout our day is preprogrammed in our brain; we are essentially operating on auto-pilot the majority of the time. Just as we learned the movements required to brush our teeth when we were a year old and now do it automatically without a second thought, we also learned from our parents, our community, and the world at large how to act in society, how to respond to certain situations, and more. We acquired our beliefs about relationships, money, security, and more from those around us; most of it by the time we were six years old. How many times has someone told you "You're just like your father?" Or you yell at your children one day out of frustration and hear your mother's words come out of your mouth.

We have learned to react to life, to circumstances in a preprogrammed way; forgetting that we have the power to determine our future just by purposefully choosing our actions in the present. It takes being mindful of our thoughts and a commitment to let go of our old habits and patterns, for we so easily slide back into what we were and how we used to do things.

How does one stay present? Ours is a world of contrasts, each day the Universe bringing us new opportunities to decide who and what we are. Are we happy or sad, angry or joyful, reactionary or calm in our response? The choice is always ours.

What if we could consciously choose a different outcome and alter the way we perceive and react to things? How would our life change? Most of us are familiar with the saying "Today is the first day of the rest of your life." Is it truly possible to wipe the slate clean every morning? Imagine what our life would look like if we consciously decided every morning how we wanted our day to unfold, what tasks we wanted to accomplish, what events we wanted to experience, all of it coming together with ease and grace. We are essentially not only in the flow with Universal energy; we are using it to co-create the life we desire. Even if we viewed yesterday as less-than-stellar, each day gives us the opportunity to begin anew, to be the highest, grandest expression of ourselves.

Living consciously is exactly that, choosing who/what we want to be, setting both our intentions and where we put our attention on a daily basis. But imagine if we applied it to each moment? What if we were to regularly step back, pause long enough to be present and decide in each moment how we are going to react to the world around us? Is it possible?

My aim this year is to live consciously. What is conscious living? For me it means mindfully choosing my actions throughout the day. Stopping along the way to decide what the next step is, what I want to create, how I want things to look. It's difficult and many times I catch myself halfway through the day and realize that I haven't given much thought to anything, that I have been pretty much on auto-pilot, scurrying around trying to get things done. Every once in a while though, I feel as if I am getting the hang of it.

My sister Moonie had a beautiful crystal pie plate with a domed cover. I had always loved it, as pies are my specialty. When she passed away, I was delighted to keep her pie plate and be reminded of her every time I used it.

Not quite sure where to store it, the pie plate sat on my kitchen counter for several weeks until one evening with guests about to arrive I carried it to the laundry room and set it on top of the washing machine. The next morning, while doing laundry, Bob (Yes, my husband does laundry!) moved the pie plate to the top of the dryer (which has a slightly rounded top), turned on the dryer and walked away.

When I heard the crash, sure enough I found Moonie's beautiful pie plate shattered on the laundry room floor. Staring at the pile of broken glass I growled at Bob, "You can clean it up!" as I stormed away. The one possession of my sister's that I really wanted to keep and my husband had carelessly broken it. I knew Bob felt terrible, but I was furious! I was not going to let him forget this one!

Within minutes though, I realized I was at a choice point. I could see myself being angry, stewing about that pie plate all day long and making Bob feel even worse. I envisioned myself savoring that anger, storing it up to use as ammunition during our next fight. Or, I could let it go. It was after all, just a pie plate. My sister was not in the pie plate; her essence, her love, was in me. Was this the emotion I wanted to attach to her pie plate? Was this the relationship I wanted with my husband?

I walked up to Bob, gave him a hug and said, "It's just a pie plate. I didn't know where to store it anyway. Don't worry about it; I know it was an accident." And surprisingly, the incident was over. The gray cloud that a minute before had hung over both of us was gone. The sun was once again shining in our home.

For me, that was a step towards conscious living. Now if I can just remember that the next time he shrinks my best sweater in the dryer.

CHAPTER 30

Love Is All There Is

"The hunger for love is much more difficult to remove than the hunger for bread."
~ Mother Teresa

I asked Kristi to write this chapter, for she is the essence of love to me. However, she refused, saying the words have to come from me. I understand, this has been, after all, my soul's journey and the lessons learned are mine.

LOVE is all there is. The most powerful force in the Universe, trumping everything else, it is God's most precious gift to us, given freely and unconditionally and available to all; our birthright. Why then do we continue to screw it up?

It begins with loving ourselves. The kiosk outside a church not too far from my home often features uplifting messages for those passing by. One particular message really caught my eye. "Jesus loves you. All of you," the sign passionately proclaimed. I interpreted "All of you" to mean "even the parts of us we feel are unlovable," for God only sees the perfection in us, knows our soul, and takes great joy in our growth and evolution.

It is only when we know true unconditional love, not the romantic type, but the kind of love that sees God's perfection in everything—every living creature in the world and beyond, even ourselves—do we begin to understand. Those who have undergone near-death experiences portray the love they sense upon entering the other dimensions as the most amazing experience, an almost indescribable feeling of peace and joy. My sister described how beautiful it felt when she was in the coma. Somewhere along the way, in the Earth plane experience, we have lost that feeling of love.

Only when we ourselves feel love are we able to appreciate that all is connected, that all is a unique aspect of God. We are unable to harm another life, whether a person, an animal, or a part of nature. We know that we are it and it is us, for God is indeed in all of us; we are all part of God's creation.

I have known unconditional love at times from my angels and guides and from my loved ones on the other side. I can feel them wrapping their arms around me, especially when I am in despair. Their love has buoyed me and kept me going when I was feeling lost and alone. I have been blessed indeed.

Love like this truly begins with us. The time is now for us to surrender those beliefs about ourselves that say we are not good enough, not loveable; to give love to both ourselves and the many others in the world just like us.

There are really only two emotions: love and fear. When we live in fear, we know hate, competition, scarcity, and lack. We buy into the idea that we are separate, the world a constant game of us versus them. There is another option though. We can send love to those people and parts of the world that are not in a frequency of love. For we understand that those who do things we deem horrifying act from a place of fear and a deep down belief that they are not loved or valued. When we let go of our fear we find the peace we are searching for.

We humans are but a mere speck in the great cosmos, yet we are powerful creators, powerful beyond anything we can imagine. What we send out to the Universe through our thoughts, words, and deeds carries an amazing energy. It ripples out across the expanse creating the exact world we see and experience.

I want to believe that we are on the cusp of a remarkable age in the history of our planet. This is a period of rebirth and renewal, a time of creation and WE are the co-creators; it is our choice point. What do we choose? Love or fear? Peace or war? Joy or sadness?

Can we recognize our divinity, our connection to all and make choices that serve and honor all life? I think we can. We agreed to come here, eager to be part of this auspicious time on planet Earth. It is time for each of us to step up and choose what kind of world we want to live in.

Deepak Chopra talks about how we can create a more peaceful world, not by marching at a peace rally or demanding our government stop the war, but by living our own lives from a place of peace, by recognizing that change begins not just with us, but in us. He believes that one by one we can reach critical mass, that we can hit that tipping point that makes peace an everyday occurrence for our entire planet.

Recently, Bob and I attended a Beatlemania concert with the local symphony. It was great fun, all of us baby boomers dancing and groovin' away to all the songs we grew up with. One thing really caught our attention though, aside from the beer bellies and blue jeans; we were delighted to see many in the audience opening their cell phones to shine light on the concert. It had been a while since we'd been to a rock concert—cell phones instead of cigarette lighters, amazing! It started with just a couple and then the lights multiplied one by one as more and more of us caught on. A single light here, another there, four more in that section, a whole row across the way. Eventually, the entire hall was filled with shining lights. Cool.

What if that was all it took? By creating harmony and light in our own life, we create harmony and light on our planet. Imagine each of us living in peace and allowing our light to shine. Can't you just see it? One by one, a twinkle here, a flicker there, until the lights begin to merge together lighting up the darkness. It kind of reminds me of the song many of us learned in Sunday school: "This Little Light of Mine, I'm Gonna Let It Shine." Sometimes it is difficult to believe that just one person can make a difference. And yes, one light is just a tiny glimmer, but thousands of lights can brighten a concert arena, and millions of lights, all shining together, can brighten a world. And guess what, it begins with just one. It begins with us.

It's in there, that beautiful spark we were born with. That bright light that declares we are a magnificent, perfect child of God, unconditionally loved and loving. We may have forgotten who we are; we may have hidden our light under a thousand shades, so dense we can barely recognize it. But it never extinguishes. It's not too late . . . to uncover our beautiful spark, to remember what brings us joy, what lights our fire, to BE who we truly are. There is only one thing to remember: *LOVE is all there is.*

CHAPTER 31

It Was All About Me

"We're not on our journey
to save the world
but to save ourselves.
But in doing that you save the world."
- Joseph Campbell

I have come to realize, as I look back on the evolution of BellaSpark, that it was all about me. The articles we have published, the speakers I have worked with, the events and workshops I have produced—were all organized because I had something to learn from these teachers. It was more about my own spiritual journey than my desire to change the world.

I have learned much on this voyage.

I know now that we are infinite beings, and when we leave this physical body, our soul lives on; enriched and wiser than before we began this incarnation.

I have learned we are always connected to Spirit and our loved ones who have transitioned to the other side and that we can contact them anytime we want. Kristi is but a thought away, and we talk often.

I have become skilled at meditating—not a small feat for one with such an active brain. It is now part of my daily practice. It allows me to connect on a regular basis with my guides, angels, and yes, Kristi. I know that I am guided and loved.

I understand that everything is energy, and what I send out to the Universe comes back to me. I like to think that I am a kinder, gentler, more compassionate person, less prone to react from past patterns and programming and able to consciously choose my words, my actions and especially my thoughts, for I am the creator of my world.

I recognize that being present is where it's at. I try to find a moment every day when I can be quiet and enjoy the feeling of utter stillness and experience the peace and joy in that precise moment. It is important to be present in the moment, for the present is all we have. I do not think about tomorrow's details or ruminate on something that happened in the past, focusing only on this present moment. Am I safe? Am I secure? It may be just a solitary moment where I can forget that which weighs me down, but I know for that instant, all is well. The chaos and drudgery of 3D physical existence may rear its head again, but for this single moment, I have peace. From that experience I create another one, and then another, until each day is filled with more and more moments such as these. I am creator of my life, consciously creating the moments—the thoughts that bring me peace and joy. One thought, one moment, one day at a time, I become my thoughts, my moments.

I realize that the answers I am seeking are not out there, but in me. I already know all that I search for; it is hardwired into my very being. My only job is to uncover it.

I have learned to trust that all is in Divine Order and to enjoy the ride.

Most of all, I have learned that it's all about love. There is no greater force in the Universe.

I appreciate that this journey is ongoing and I am never done; there is always more to learn, to experience. I know that each of us is a Divine spark of light and our number one purpose is to live that light.

I honor Kristi not by being her voice, but by being mine, by living life fully and embracing the initiations of the soul—the pain as well as the joy—and by letting go of my fears and stepping into my authentic self. I have come to understand that we are all limitless spiritual beings, powerful beyond belief. I am no longer willing to play small, to be less-than. My daughter spoke her truth, and I am committed to being more like her; she showed me the way. Her life and death were the catalyst for me to follow my path to my own greatness. I did find Kristi, but more importantly, I found myself.

I have learned to be resilient since the death of my child, to draw on an inner strength I wasn't aware I had. Today I choose to face life head on by experiencing every minute of it, both the sorrow and the joy. This incredible play is my life, and I live it to the fullest. I let The Mask go for good. *Thank you for sharing my journey with me and for being a beautiful spark, igniting change in your own special way.*

It has been ten years now since my daughter left. Once again we are painting our house, only this time we fill the brush strokes with love and joy.

I have come to realize that the mountain I have been searching for is not a place, it is the journey. I was in a deep, deep valley when Kristi left, and I have been climbing that mountain for ten long years. Kristi did meet me at the base of the mountain, and she has been at my side every step of the way, guiding me, encouraging me, urging me forward, loving me and holding me safe. Along the way I have been blessed to experience wonderful people and amazing adventures.

The Dream . . .

It's been a long time since Kristi has shown up in one of my dreams:

We are walking hand-in-hand up the side of a mountain. We reach the peak and look back. I see the winding and sometimes treacherous path we navigated stretching out for miles behind us.

We look around at the expansive vista before us and observe the lush green valley far below. The sun is shining and the world is huge and welcoming.

Kristi holds out her hand. "Do you trust me?"

I nod and take her hand.

We step off the side of the mountain and soar.

Appendix

I have met many wonderful authors, speakers, and teachers throughout this journey. I humbly thank each and every one of them. Some of them know how much I value their wisdom and insight and others do not have a clue how much they impacted my life.

As a thank you, I have listed all of them and their websites for your easy access.

Alexander, Dr. Eben – *www.lifebeyonddeath.net*
Batista, Sarina – *SarinaBaptista.com*
Beckwith, Michael Bernard – *www.agapelive.com*
Beckwith, Rickie Byars – *www.rickiebyarsbeckwith.com*
Borysenko, Joan – *www.joanborysenko.com*
Braden, Gregg – *www.greggbraden.com*
Browne, Sylvia – *www.sylviabrowne.com*
Chopra, Deepak – *www.deepakchopra.com*
Choquette, Sonia – *www.soniachoquette.com*
Cohen, Alan – *www.alancohen.com*
Crowther, Kiesha — Little Grandmother –
www.littlegrandmother.com
Dispenza, Dr. Joe – *www.drjoedispenza.com*
Dyer, Dr. Wayne – *www.drwaynedyer.com*
Fredrick, Sue – w*ww.careerintuitive.com*
Freke, Timothy – *www.timothyfreke.com*
Giesemann, Suzanne – *www.suzannegiesemann.com*
Gossett, Louis – *www.louisgossett.com*
Gutierrez, Daniel – *www.danielgutierrez.com*

Harris, Lee – *www.leeharrisenergy.com*
Holland, John – *www.johnholland.com*
Hoppe, Geoff and Linda – *www.crimsoncircle.com*
Hubbard, Barbara Marx – *www.barbaramarxhubbard.com*
James, Cynthia – *www.cynthiajames.net*
Kieves, Tama – *www.tamakieves.com*
Kinkade, Amelia – *www.ameliakinkade.com*
Lipton, Bruce – *www.brucelipton.com*
Maa, Sai – *www.sai-maa.com*
MacLaine, Shirley – *www.shirleymaclaine.com*
McElroy, Margaret – *www.margaretmcelroy.com*
McTaggart, Lynne – *www.lynnmctaggart.com*
Myss, Caroline – *www.myss.com*
Northrop, Suzane – *www.suzanenorthrop.com*
Peters, Cash – *www.cashpeters.com*
Quinn, Gary – *www.garyquinn.tv*
Redfield, James – *www.celestinevision.com*
Renard, Gary – *www.garyrenard.com*
Rose, Kimmie – *www.kimmierose.com*
Ross, Merrie Lynn – *www.merrieway.com*
Ruiz, don Miguel – *www.miguelruiz.com*
Sha, Master Zhi Gang – *www.drsha.com*
Self, Jim – *www.masteringalchemy.com*
Twyman, James – *www.jamestwyman.com*
Van Praagh, James – *www.vanpraagh.com*
Vanzant, Iyanla – *www.innervisionsworldwide.com*
Virtue, Doreen – *www.angeltherapy.com*
Walsch, Neale Donald – *www.nealedonaldwalsch.com*
Weiss, Brian – *www.brianweiss.com*
Williamson, Marianne – *www.marianne.com*
Zukav, Gary – *www.seatofthesoul.com*

About Donna

Donna Visocky is the founder of BellaSpark Productions and publisher of *BellaSpark Magazine.* One of the top metaphysical and consciousness-raising organizations in the United States, BellaSpark was named after Donna's daughter Kristi who died in an automobile accident in 2003. Kristi was a beautiful spark and passionate about creating change. It was her passing that propelled Donna on her soul journey.

BellaSpark's mission is to be a catalyst; to stimulate, inspire and embolden individuals and communities in their growing spiritual awareness by providing access to consciousness raising ideas, people, and information. For the past ten years, Donna has met, interviewed, and facilitated conversations with hundreds of the world's top visionaries, change-makers, speakers, artists, and musicians who bring their gifts and talents to help our individual spark to grow. Donna also co-hosts a weekly radio show, *InnerViews with Kimmie Rose and Donna Visocky* on CBS Sky Radio.

Donna has over 20 years experience in non-profit work, business management and event planning. According to Donna, "She has been training her entire life for this role." Through BellaSpark, she honors her daughter's memory by celebrating the beautiful, passionate spark of inspiration she knew her to be.

Donna resides in Colorado with her husband Bob, close to her children and three grandchildren, the lights of her life.

Kristi Visocky Memorial Foundation

The tide recedes, but leaves behind,
bright seashells on the sand.
The sun goes down, but gentle warmth,
still lingers on the land.
The music stops, and yet it echoes on
in sweet refrain . . .
For every joy that passes,
something beautiful remains.
- Author Unknown

The Kristi Visocky Memorial Foundation, a.k.a. Kristi's Fund, was created in memory of Kristi Visocky who was killed in an auto accident in May of 2003 at the age of 21. Determined to keep alive the spirit and compassion of a young woman who was a strong champion of the underdog and supporter of troubled youth, Kristi's Fund was created to provide scholarships to young women and assistance to area programs.

Since it's inception in 2003 the Kristi Visocky Memorial Foundation has:

- Awarded $200,000 in scholarships to 90 young women
- Donated $40,000 to area organizations supporting women and families
- Provided Thanksgiving Meals for those in need

Current projects include building a Habitat for Humanity House. *The House that Kristi Built: Celebrating Community* will be built in spring 2014.

Kristi's Fund is supported through the generous donations of community businesses and individuals. The annual Kristi Visocky Memorial Golf Tournament and Big Night Out provide significant financial support for the organization.

"We are eternally grateful to this amazing community who has gathered around us to help create beautiful beginnings from the ashes of grief." Bob Visocky

The Kristi Visocky Memorial Foundation is a 501c3 organization.
Tax I.D. Number: 20-3090528

For more information or to donate: **www.kristisfund.com**